LAW, CRIME AND LAW ENFORCEMENT

LEGALITIES OF GPS AND CELL PHONE SURVEILLANCE

LAW, CRIME AND LAW ENFORCEMENT

Additional books in this series can be found on Nova's website under the Series tab.

Additional E-books in this series can be found on Nova's website under the e-books tab.

LAWS AND LEGISLATION

Additional books in this series can be found on Nova's website under the Series tab.

Additional E-books in this series can be found on Nova's website under the e-books tab.

LAW, CRIME AND LAW ENFORCEMENT

LEGALITIES OF GPS AND CELL PHONE SURVEILLANCE

EMILY M. JOHNSON
AND
MICHAEL J. RODRIGUEZ
EDITORS

NOVINKA

New York

For permission to use material from this book please contact us:
Telephone 631-231-7269; Fax 631-231-8175
Web Site: http://www.novapublishers.com

Additional color graphics may be available in the e-book version of this book.

LIBRARY OF CONGRESS CATALOGING-IN-PUBLICATION DATA

ISBN: 978-1-62257-026-3

Published by Nova Science Publishers, Inc. † New York

CONTENTS

PREFACE

As technology continues to advance, what was once thought novel, even a luxury, quickly becomes commonplace, even a necessity. Global Positioning System (GPS) technology is one such example. Generally, GPS is a satellite-based technology that discloses the location of a given object. This technology is used in automobiles and cell phones to provide individual drivers with directional assistance. Just as individuals are finding increasing applications for GPS technology, state and federal governments are as well. State and federal law enforcement use various forms of GPS technology to obtain evidence in criminal investigations. For example, federal prosecutors have used information from cellular phone service providers that allows real-time tracking of the locations of customers' cellular phones. This book discusses the basics of GPS technology, society's reliance on it, and some of the related legal and privacy implications, with a focus on the legislative and judicial responses on both the federal and state levels.

Chapter 1 - As technology continues to advance, what was once thought novel, even a luxury, quickly becomes commonplace, even a necessity. Global Positioning System (GPS) technology is one such example. Generally, GPS is a satellite-based technology that discloses the location of a given object. This technology is used in automobiles and cell phones to provide individual drivers with directional assistance. Just as individuals are finding increasing applications for GPS technology, state and federal governments are as well. State and federal law enforcement use various forms of GPS technology to obtain evidence in criminal investigations. For example, federal prosecutors have used information from cellular phone service providers that allows real-time tracking of the locations of customers' cellular phones. Title III of the Omnibus Crime Control and Safe Streets Act of 1958 (P.L. 90-351) regulates the interception of wire, oral, and electronic communications. As such, it does not regulate the use of GPS technology affixed to vehicles and is beyond the scope of this report. However, bills introduced in the 112th Congress, such as S. 1212 and H.R. 2168, would address circumstances under which law enforcement may obtain, use, or disclose GPS data.

Chapter 2 - Technology has advanced considerably since the framers established the constitutional parameters for searches and seizures in the Fourth Amendment. What were ink quills and parchment are now cell phones and the Internet. It is undeniable that these advances in technology threaten to diminish privacy. Law enforcement's use of cell phones and GPS devices to track an individual's movements brings into sharp relief the challenge of reconciling technology, privacy, and law. Beyond the Constitution, a miscellany of statutes and cases may apply to these tracking activities. One such statute is the Electronic Communications Privacy Act of 1986 (ECPA), P.L. 99-508, 100 Stat. 1848 (1986), which protects individual privacy and governs the methods by which law enforcement may retrieve electronic communications information for investigative purposes, including pen registers, trap and trace devices, wiretaps, and tracking devices. The primary debate surrounding cell phone and GPS tracking is not whether they are permitted by statute but rather what legal standard should apply: probable cause, reasonable suspicion, or something less.

Chapter 3 - In United States v. Jones, 132 S. Ct. 945 (2012), all nine Supreme Court Justices agreed that Jones was searched when the police attached a Global Positioning System (GPS) device to the undercarriage of his car and tracked his movements for four weeks. The Court, however, splintered on what constituted the search: the attachment of the device or the long-term monitoring. The majority held that the attachment of the GPS device and an attempt to obtain information was the violation; Justice Alito, concurring, argued that the monitoring was a violation of Jones's reasonable expectation of privacy; and Justice Sotomayor, also concurring, agreed with them both, but would provide further Fourth Amendment protections. This report will examine these three decisions in an effort to find their place in the body of existing Fourth Amendment law pertaining to privacy, property, and technology.

Chapter 4 - The Government obtained a search warrant permitting it to install a Global-Positioning-System (GPS) tracking device on a vehicle registered to respondent Jones's wife. The warrant authorized installation in the District of Columbia and within 10 days, but agents in-stalled the device on the 11th day and in Maryland. The Government then tracked the vehicle's movements for 28 days. It subsequently secured an indictment of Jones and others on drug trafficking conspiracy charges. The District Court suppressed the GPS data obtained while the vehicle was parked at Jones's residence, but held the remaining data admissible because Jones had no reasonable expectation of privacy when the vehicle was on public streets. Jones was convicted. The D. C. Circuit reversed, concluding that admission of the evidence obtained by warrantless use of the GPS device violated the Fourth Amendment.

In: Legalities of GPS and Cell Phone Surveillance ISBN: 978-1-62257-026-3
Editors: E. Johnson and M. Rodriguez

Chapter 1

LAW ENFORCEMENT USE OF GLOBAL POSITIONING (GPS) DEVICES TO MONITOR MOTOR VEHICLES: FOURTH AMENDMENT CONSIDERATIONS*

Alison M. Smith

SUMMARY

As technology continues to advance, what was once thought novel, even a luxury, quickly becomes commonplace, even a necessity. Global Positioning System (GPS) technology is one such example. Generally, GPS is a satellite-based technology that discloses the location of a given object. This technology is used in automobiles and cell phones to provide individual drivers with directional assistance. Just as individuals are finding increasing applications for GPS technology, state and federal governments are as well. State and federal law enforcement use various forms of GPS technology to obtain evidence in criminal investigations. For example, federal prosecutors have used information from cellular phone service providers that allows real-time tracking of the locations of customers' cellular phones. Title III of the Omnibus Crime Control and Safe Streets Act of 1958 (P.L. 90-351) regulates

* This is an edited, reformatted and augmented version of the Congressional Research Service Publication, CRS Report for Congress R41663, dated November 22, 2011.

the interception of wire, oral, and electronic communications. As such, it does not regulate the use of GPS technology affixed to vehicles and is beyond the scope of this report. However, bills introduced in the 112th Congress, such as S. 1212 and H.R. 2168, would address circumstances under which law enforcement may obtain, use, or disclose GPS data.

The increased reliance on GPS technology raises important societal and legal considerations. Some contend that law enforcement's use of such technology to track motor vehicles' movements provides for a safer society. Conversely, others have voiced concerns that GPS technology could be used to reveal information inherently private. Defendants on both the state and federal levels are raising Fourth Amendment constitutional challenges, asking the courts to require law enforcement to first obtain a warrant before using GPS technology.

Subject to a few exceptions, the Fourth Amendment of the U.S. Constitution requires law enforcement to obtain a warrant before conducting a search or making a seizure. Courts continue to grapple with the specific issue of whether law enforcement's use of GPS technology constitutes a search or seizure, as well as the broader question of how the Constitution should address advancing technology in general. The Supreme Court may provide some answers in *United States v. Jones* (131 S.Ct. 3064 (2011)) when it addresses the issue of whether law enforcement's use of GPS technology in connection with motor vehicles falls within the Fourth Amendment's purview. Lower federal courts have arrived at varying conclusions. Several district and circuit courts of appeals have concluded that law enforcement's current use of GPS technology does not constitute a search, and is thus permissible, under the Constitution. One circuit court has found the duration of GPS tracking to be constitutionally significant. State legislatures and state courts have approached the issue in various ways. Some states have enacted laws requiring law enforcement to obtain a warrant before using GPS technology. Some state courts have resolved the question under their own constitutions. Other state courts have relied on Supreme Court precedent, such as *United States v. Knotts*, 460 U.S. 276 (1983), to derive an answer.

This report discusses the basics of GPS technology, society's reliance on it, and some of the related legal and privacy implications. In addition, the report examines legislative and judicial responses on both federal and state levels.

GLOBAL POSITIONING SYSTEM (GPS) TECHNOLOGY

GPS "is a satellite-based technology that reveals information about the location, speed, and direction of a targeted subject. While it was initially developed for the U.S. military, countless civilian applications of GPS appear in the marketplace."[1] For example, many people rely on an automotive GPS device when they travel[2] for navigational directions, or even to find dining options. Similarly, some companies equip their vehicles with built-in GPS devices that allow a command center to know a vehicle's location upon its involvement in an accident or track it if it is stolen.[3] Pet collars have been outfitted with GPS devices to enable owners to locate their lost pets.[4] Campers and hikers use portable GPS devices to determine their location and map out their journey.[5] Cellular phones are embedded with GPS devices to synchronize time changes when a person leaves a certain time zone.[6] Cartographers use GPS devices to make maps and surveyors to determine property boundaries.[7] Airlines use them to pilot and locate planes.[8] In short, not only are Americans finding an increased interest in GPS technology, but it is becoming an essential aspect of many Americans' day-to-day lives.[9]

Law Enforcement's Uses of GPS Technology

The military and private sector are not alone in their interests and reliance on GPS technology. Federal and state governments have also incorporated it into many of their domestic activities. Examples include tracking stranded motorists and predicting natural disasters such as earthquakes, tsunamis, hurricanes, etc. Such tracking allows for more effective emergency preparedness and relief to victims.[10]

Increasingly, law enforcement relies on and finds new uses for GPS technology to assist in monitoring and gathering evidence.[11] For example, sex offenders are outfitted with ankle monitors to track their movements 24 hours a day. Also, consider the following examples, taken by various state law enforcement authorities:

- After 11 attacks on women were reported during a six-month period in two Virginia counties, police installed a GPS device on the van owned by a man who lived near the crime scenes. The suspect was a convicted rapist who had served 17 years in prison. By tracking his movements with the device, police were able to intercept him in Falls

Church, VA, where he was dragging a woman to a remote area. The series of assaults ceased after his arrest.[12]

- Wisconsin police, acting on a tip about a former methamphetamine manufacturer, attached a GPS device to the suspect's car without first obtaining a warrant. Information recorded on the device led them to a large tract of land visited by the suspect. With the consent of the landowner, they searched the property and found paraphernalia used to manufacture methamphetamines. The suspect was subsequently arrested.[13]
- Police in New York used evidence acquired from a GPS device (attached without first obtaining a warrant) that had been attached to a burglary suspect's car a year earlier. The device, which monitored the suspect's movement without interruption for more than two months, showed that the suspect had driven by a burglarized store. This evidence was used to corroborate a witness's testimony that the suspect had been observing the store to determine its vulnerable points.[14]
- In California, the Los Angeles Police Department "outfit[ted] its cruisers with air guns that can launch GPS-enabled 'darts' at passing cars."[15] Once affixed to a vehicle, police can track it in real time from police headquarters. The air guns are generally used in situations requiring immediate action such as a high-speedchase.[16]

Most new cellular phones include GPS capabilities.[17] As a result, federal prosecutors have been known to get information from cellular phone service providers that allows real time tracking of the locations of customers' cellular phones.[18] In one case, information obtained from a cellular phone's GPS helped prove that a key suspect had been within a mile of a murder scene. In another case, a Mexican drug-cartel truck was tracked. The truck was carrying over two tons of cocaine.[19]

While there are many substantial benefits to the use of GPS technology, some have voiced concerns. Many of these concerns arise from law enforcement's use of GPS technology without first obtaining a warrant to either attach the device or monitor the suspect after the device has been attached. Some have argued that the warrantless use of GPS technology has the potential of interfering with individual privacy, protected by the Fourth Amendment to the United States Constitution.[20] Legal scholars assert that a warrant ensures that the police have probable cause to believe that criminal activity is taking place or is imminent, thus preventing unwarranted intrusion into a person's freedom and private life.[21] Others contend that GPS tracking is analogous to law enforcement conducting public surveillance with its own eyes or with surveillance cameras or radio transmitting beepers. Therefore, some courts and legal scholars believe a warrant is unnecessary and the Fourth Amendment does not apply.[22]

THE FOURTH AMENDMENT

The Fourth Amendment to the United States Constitution, which protects "[t]he right of the people to be secure ... against unreasonable searches and seizures,"[23] governs and circumscribes searches and seizures[24] made by the federal and the state governments.[25] The Amendment's operative text can be divided into two clauses. The first clause forbids the government from conducting any search or seizure that is "unreasonable." The second clause prohibits the government from issuing a warrant unless it is obtained based "upon probable cause," is "supported by Oath," and contains particularized descriptions of the "place to be searched" and what is "to be seized." Although "[t]here is nothing in the amendment's text to suggest that a warrant is required to make a search or seizure reasonable,"[26] the U.S. Supreme Court has long since read these two clauses together, generally holding that a warrantless search or seizure is presumptively (if not per se) unreasonable.[27] The Fourth Amendment does not apply, however, unless the government's conduct constitutes a search or seizure within the meaning of the Amendment, that is, where there is a justifiable expectation of privacy. In addition, even when the Amendment does apply, "because the ultimate touchstone of the Fourth Amendment is 'reasonableness,' the warrant requirement is subject to certain exceptions."[28]

At one time, the purpose of the Fourth Amendment was seen as a protection of people's property rights against unlawful physical trespasses.[29] However, it gradually came to be seen as a protection of something more.[30] "[T]he principal object of the Fourth Amendment," the Court has explained, "is the protection of privacy rather than property."[31] In addition, "the Fourth Amendment protects people—and not simply 'areas'—against unreasonable searches and seizures."[32] Thus, in its seminal decision in *Katz v. United States*,[33] the Court held that police officers violated the Fourth Amendment when they conducted a warrantless search using a listening and recording device placed on the outside of a public phone booth to eavesdrop on the conversation of a suspect who had "'justifiably relied' upon ... [the privacy of the] telephone booth."[34] The Court concluded that the Fourth Amendment protects both a person and that person's expectation of privacy from warrantless searches or seizures in places which are justifiably believed to be private.

It is not enough, however, for a person to have a subjective "expectation of privacy," for any person might claim that she expected privacy at any time and in any place. Indeed, many might argue that the police conduct a search by simply watching them. Therefore, they will reason, because the police did not have a warrant, they violated the Constitution and the evidence obtained cannot be used against them.[35] However, the Court has rejected such broad interpretations of the term "search," holding instead "that visual observation is no 'search' at all."[36] Simply put, "the police cannot reasonably be expected to avert their eyes from ... activity that could have been observed by any member of the public. Hence, '[w]hat a person knowingly exposes to the public, even in his own home or office, is not a subject of Fourth Amendment protection.'"[37]

In applying the principles set forth in *Katz* to determine whether law enforcement has conducted a search or a seizure within the meaning of the Fourth Amendment, the Court frequently cites *Katz*'s concurring opinion. The concurring opinion clarified the Court's test as being "whether a person has a 'constitutionally protected reasonable expectation of privacy.'"[38] Courts presently examine law enforcement's conduct to make this threshold determination by following "a two-part inquiry: first, has the individual manifested a subjective expectation of privacy in the object of the challenged search? Second, is society willing to recognize that expectation as reasonable?"[39]

The Fourth Amendment and Technology

State and federal courts have long since wrestled with whether and how to apply the *Katz* test to advancing technology. For example, the Supreme Court in *Katz* determined that when the suspect entered the phone booth and shut the door, he had a reasonable expectation of privacy that his telephone conversation would be private. Thus, the police conducted an unreasonable search by using a listening and recording device without getting a warrant. Similarly, in *Kyllo v. United States*,[40] the Court decided that a suspect had a reasonable expectation of privacy in his home when the police, suspecting him of growing marijuana, used a thermal imaging device without a warrant to detect the heat emanating from it. In contrast, when the Court was asked in *United States v. Ciraolo*[41] to decide whether a suspect had a reasonable expectation of privacy in a back yard he surrounded with a 10-foot-high fence, the Court concluded that police observation from an airplane in public air space was not a search; thus, no warrant was necessary.

Likewise, the Court found that a defendant did not have a reasonable expectation of privacy in his car while traveling along public roads. In *United States v. Knotts,*[42] Minnesota law enforcement officers placed (with the seller's consent) a beeper in a chloroform container, believing that the defendant buyer was engaging in the production of illicit drugs. Officers subsequently followed the vehicle carrying the container, maintaining both a visual surveillance and a monitor receiving the beeper signals. Based on the beeper signals, the officers tracked the container to the defendant's secluded cabin. After a three-day visual surveillance of the cabin, the officers obtained and executed a search warrant and found the container and a drug laboratory in the cabin. The defendant sought to have the evidence suppressed, arguing that the warrantless monitoring of the beeper violated the Fourth Amendment.

The Court disagreed and held that the officers' actions did not constitute a search or seizure, as the defendant did not have a legitimate expectation of privacy. The beeper signal was not used to monitor movement of the container within a private residence. Instead, it was used to monitor movement along public highways and other areas visible to the naked eye.

However, in a similar scenario, when a beeper was activated while inside various suspects' homes, the Court held that suspects with interests in those respective homes did have a reasonable expectation of privacy and that the absence of a warrant constituted an unreasonable search.[43] In *United States v. Karo,*[44] Drug Enforcement Administration (DEA) agents installed an electronic beeper in a can of ether with the consent of the owner (a government informant). The marked can was sold with others to the defendants, who intended to use the contents for cocaine production. Having tracked the can to several residences and storage facilities, law enforcement determined the can's location and obtained an arrest warrant. The defendants were arrested and charged with possession of cocaine with intent to distribute. One of the defendants sought to have the evidence suppressed as "tainted fruit" of an unlawful search. This case presented two issues for the Court to address: (1) whether the beeper's installation constituted a search or seizure when the container was delivered to a buyer without any knowledge of the beeper's presence and (2) whether the beeper's monitoring within an individual's residence falls within the Fourth Amendment's ambit when it reveals information that could not have been obtained through visual surveillance.

As to the first issue, the Court found that the defendant lacked a Fourth Amendment interest, as the then-owner's consent was sufficient to withstand the challenge. [45] However, the Court found that the Fourth Amendment was violated when the agents used the beeper to locate the container in a private dwelling without first obtaining a search warrant. Although the transfer of the beeper to the defendant did not violate the Fourth Amendment, the monitoring of the beeper in a private residence not open to visual surveillance did violate the Fourth Amendment.[46]

GPS Monitoring: States' Responses

States have employed various approaches toward the use of GPS technology. Some states have addressed the issue statutorily by enacting laws "imposing civil and criminal penalties for the [improper] use of electronic tracking devices or expressly requiring exclusion of evidence produced by such a device unless obtained by the police acting pursuant to a warrant."[47] Judicially, state courts have reached differing conclusions. State courts in New York, Washington, Oregon, Delaware, and Massachusetts have determined that, absent some exigent circumstance, police officers must first obtain a warrant before using GPS technology (in some cases the court is interpreting its respective state constitution).[48] For example, in *State v. Weaver*,[49] the Court of Appeals of New York held that the "unconsented placement" of a GPS tracking device and subsequent monitoring of the vehicle constituted a search requiring a warrant under the state's constitution.[50] The court noted that it has interpreted its constitution to provide greater protections than the Fourth Amendment "in the areas of search and seizure."[51] The court found that the defendant had a reasonable expectation of privacy that was infringed by the state's action. While the court found that the defendant had a diminished expectation of privacy, "that expectation was not reduced to zero."

Conversely, state courts in Nevada and Virginia have found that GPS use does not raise any state or federal constitutional concerns.[52] In *Foltz v. Commonwealth*,[53] the Virginia court found that the law enforcement's use of a GPS tracking device to track a vehicle's movement on a public street did not constitute a search or seizure under either the federal or state constitutions. The defendant, a registered sex offender on probation for committing sexual assault, became a suspect in a new series of sexual assaults. Police attached a

GPS device to the defendant's work vehicle. Observing "in real time via a computer screen with a map,"[54] police noticed that the van was driven in and out of various neighborhoods where crimes had occurred. After another sexual assault occurred, the police followed the defendant the next day and witnessed him grab a woman and knock her down to the ground. The police stopped the assault and arrested the defendant. In reaching its decision, the court concluded that the defendant did not manifest a subjective expectation of privacy while driving down the street looking for victims. Moreover, the court concluded that the defendant "did nothing to prevent others from inspecting the bumper of the work van." Many states have not addressed the issue of GPS tracking either legislatively or judicially as of this writing.

GPS MONITORING: FEDERAL COURTS

The Supreme Court has not directly addressed the issue of whether law enforcement's use of GPS technology in connection with motor vehicles falls within the Fourth Amendment's purview. Lower federal courts have relied on Supreme Court precedent on other types of monitoring to arrive at arguably varying conclusions on GPS tracking.

Several district and circuit courts of appeals have concluded that law enforcement's current use of GPS technology does not constitute a search and is thus permissible under the Constitution.[55] For example, in *United States v. Pineda-Moreno*,[56] the 9th Circuit decided a case involving a criminal drug investigation in Oregon. Without a warrant, DEA agents attached a GPS device to a Jeep owned by a man suspected of drug activity. The device was attached on several occasions over a four-month period.[57] Four times agents attached the device while the Jeep was parked on a public street; one time while it was parked at a public parking lot; and two times while it was parked on his property, necessitating that agents sneak onto it in the early morning hours.[58] Eventually, the GPS "device alerted agents that [the suspect's] vehicle was leaving a suspected marijuana grow site." The suspect was then arrested and officers found marijuana in the Jeep.[59]

The court held that the DEA's actions did not constitute a search because a person does not have a reasonable expectation of privacy in a car's exterior, even when the car is parked on the person's driveway (unless the person has affirmatively sought to exclude others from entering his land).[60] The court then held that the DEA's monitoring of the suspect's travel was analogous to the facts in *Knotts*, where the police followed the suspect's car by using a beeper on the theory that using the GPS device disclosed information that the police "could have obtained by following the car."[61] The court then concluded by quoting *Knotts*: "'Insofar as [Pineda-Moreno's] complaint appears to be simply that scientific devices such as the [tracking devices] enabled the police to be more effective in detecting crime, it simply has no constitutional foundation. We have never equated police efficiency with unconstitutionality and decline to do so now.'"[62]

Similar to *Pineda-Moreno*, many of the courts to follow this line of reasoning also have analogized GPS devices to the beeper devices in *Knotts*. In addition, many have also included a reservation similar to the one the Supreme Court made in *Knotts*. In *Knotts*, the defendant argued that the Court's ruling would permit the government to conduct warrantless and unlimited surveillance with such technology: "[I]f such dragnet type law enforcement practices as the defendant envisions should eventually occur," the Court responded, "there will be time enough then to determine whether different constitutional principles may be applicable."[63] It is unclear what this "dragnet reservation" means, and the differing outcomes in the federal circuits can be attributed to how the courts interpret it. The 9th Circuit, quoting with approval the 7th Circuit, stated it this way: "Should [the] government someday decide to institute programs of mass surveillance of vehicular movements, it will be time enough to decide whether the Fourth Amendment should be interpreted to treat such surveillance as a search."[64]

Conversely, the D.C. Circuit held that law enforcement's prolonged use of GPS technology to track a particular vehicle does amount to a search and thus requires a warrant.[65] In *United States v. Maynard*,[66] the court found that *Knotts*'s "dragnet warning" applied to an individual when the law enforcement's warrantless surveillance was constant and protracted, and that the reservation was not limited to mass surveillance of multiple vehicles. In this case, the Federal Bureau of Investigation (FBI) installed a GPS device on a vehicle to track the "movements" of a club owner suspected of conspiracy to distribute cocaine. They monitored him "[for] 24 hours a day for 28 days as he moved among scores of places, thereby discovering the totality and pattern of his movements from place to place to place."[67] The information was subsequently used as evidence at trial to prove his involvement in the conspiracy.[68]

The court distinguished its holding from the decisions in the other circuits by noting that the rule in *Knotts* was limited. Whereas the other circuits had read *Knotts*'s dragnet reservation to mean "mass surveillance," the court read it to apply as well to individual, prolonged "'twenty-four hour surveillance.'"[69]

The court also concluded that a person has a reasonable expectation of privacy in the totality of his movements over the course of a month, which he does not actually or constructively expose to the public, even though law enforcement could constitutionally conduct warrantless observation of his individual movements from one place to another while in public.[70] The Supreme Court granted certiorari review in this case[71] raising questions as to whether and when the warrantless use of a GPS tracking device on a motor vehicle might violate the Fourth Amendment.

Differing Decisions

Reading the decisions to date, it is unclear whether there is a split in Fourth Amendment jurisprudence over use of GPS technology as such, or the cases reflect more that differences in the extent of GPS tracking may be constitutionally significant in determining its intrusiveness. A few courts may go so far as to conclude that any use of GPS technology, even when attaching it, is presumptively unreasonable unless law enforcement first obtains a valid warrant.[72] Other courts may decide that the warrantless use of GPS technology is permissible, subject to one of the already settled warrant exceptions, such as when the suspect is fleeing and the police are engaged in hot pursuit. The state court decisions in Washington, Oregon, and New York seem to have adopted this approach under their own constitutions. Finally, some courts may argue, which could be seen as an attempt to reconcile the already existing decisions, that using GPS devices for a minimal amount of time—for a few days, perhaps—is permissible, but when the monitoring becomes prolonged—for many days, weeks, or months—the intrusiveness reaches a point where it becomes a search requiring a warrant.[73] The state court's decision in New York might also be read this way, and the D.C. Circuit appears to have followed this approach.[74]

Competing Interests

In approaching warrantless use of GPS technology, courts confront the continued appropriateness of a principal corollary of Fourth Amendment doctrine. Fourth Amendment protection is premised on a reasonable expectation of privacy that society is willing to recognize. For decades, and in a variety of circumstances, courts have held that no privacy rights attach to activities that are visually observable to the public, such as movements along public streets. The pressure on this principle comes from the greatly enhanced reach and efficiency of tracking technologies such as GPS. Some contend that it would be better for legislatures rather than the courts to set the rules on GPS policy because they can more expressly balance the competing interests of enhancing law enforcement efficiency and protection of individual privacy.[75] Others argue that the courts are capable and equipped to do it, just as they have done reconciling the law to the usage of many other emerging technologies.[76]

Those who argue that law enforcement does not need to obtain a warrant to use GPS technology contend that the many uses of GPS technology simply "enable[] the police to be more effective in detecting crime,"[77] stamping it out at its earlier stages and preventing it from even occurring. Among others, the advantages in such technology, especially when police officers are engaged in a high-speed chase, decrease the likelihood of endangering the public, the police, or even the suspect from the potential hazards involved in such situations. Moreover, as already discussed, the efficiencies of GPS technology have enabled officers to prevent one woman from being raped and any further rapes from being committed by the suspect. Likewise, proponents of GPS use maintain that officers have been able to prevent drug production and distribution by the respective suspects they apprehended. GPS technology, then, can be preventive, saving lives and time; it decreases the cost of having officers out conducting surveillance while simultaneously allowing more places and people to be monitored and more action to be taken when criminal activity occurs. In short, from this perspective, GPS devices make law enforcement's job more efficient, safer, and effective, providing for a securer and safer society. They would argue that GPS technology functions "merely as an enhancing adjunct to the surveilling officer's eyes,"[78] and naked eye observation does not offend the Fourth Amendment because a person does not have a reasonable expectation of privacy in activity that any member of the public might observe. GPS technology is merely a matter of efficiency, they conclude, and the courts "have never equated police efficiency with unconstitutionality."[79]

Conversely, proponents of requiring law enforcement to obtain judicial permission before using a GPS device contend that efficiency, security, and safety come at some unacceptable costs.[80] At "the press of a button," for example, a GPS device can disclose one's activities that are "indisputably private [in] nature," such as "trips to the psychiatrist, the plastic surgeon, the abortion clinic, the AIDS treatment center, the strip club, the criminal defense attorney, the by-the-hour motel, the union meeting, the mosque, synagogue or church, the gay bar and on and on."[81] It does not only disclose "where we go, but by easy reference [it reveals] our associations—political, religious, amicable and amorous," as well as "the pattern of our professional and avocational pursuits."[82] GPS technology "is not a mere enhancement of human sensory capacity," because the information it can capture is potentially tantamount to, "at a minimum, millions of additional police officers and cameras on every street lamp."[83] A person does have a reasonable expectation of privacy from the government's ability to obtain such comprehensive and detailed information. The ability of the government to engage in monitoring that exposes this type of information, some even argue, foreshadows "Orwellian images of Big Brother secretly following your movements through the small device in your pocket"[84] or car, especially when the pervasive monitoring has been prolonged and continuous—for 28[85] and even 65[86] days, in certain cases. Besides, they contend, unless the situation is an emergency, it is not that onerous a burden to require the police to take a few minutes to obtain judicial approval before they use such revealing technology.[87]

CONCLUSION

Society's increased reliance on GPS technology raises both societal and legal considerations. Law enforcement has found many uses for GPS technology in criminal investigations. Some of these uses in connection with motor vehicle surveillance raise concerns over the technology's potential interference with privacy interests protected by the Fourth Amendment. Others have argued that GPS technology is comparable to naked eye observation, and its advantages in impeding and preventing criminal activity are substantial. However, others contend that balancing the privacy and law enforcement interests is not easy in a GPS context. There are also questions as to whether guidance of GPS use should be provided legislatively or judicially. It is important to note that the Fourth Amendment provides a floor for protection. No matter what the state legislatures or Congress does, the requirements of the Fourth Amendment must be met. Legislation provides two advantages: (1) clarification for procedural distinctions between warrantless and presumptively unreasonable searches, and (2) additional protection where reenforcement is thought necessary. Several state legislatures have enacted legislation governing the warrantless use of GPS devices. On the federal level, bills, such as S. 1212 and H.R. 2168, in part, delineate circumstances under which law enforcement may use, obtain, or disclose GPS information.

The Supreme Court is poised to speak to the use of GPS monitoring in Spring 2012 in *United States v. Jones*. State and lower federal courts have reached differing conclusions based on the facts presented, U.S. Supreme Court precedent on other tracking devices, and/or state constitutions.

End Notes

[1] Renee McDonald Hutchins, *Tied Up in Knotts? GPS Technology and the Fourth Amendment*, 55 UCLA L. Rev. 409, 414 (2007); *see also* the Global Positioning System, http://www.gps.gov.

[2] *See* Global Positioning System, Roads & Highways, http://www.gps.gov/applications/roads. One brand name example is a TomTom. The individual can enter into the device an address, and an automated voice, along with interactive maps, will guide the driver. *See* TomTom, How Does GPS Work?, http://www.tomtom.com/howdoesitwork/index.php?Language=1.

[3] *See, e.g.*, OnStar, Our Privacy Practices, Effective January 1, 2011, https://www.onstar.com/web/portal/privacy#Header. OnStar provides other limited circumstances when it will track the location of the vehicle, such as an in-car request for service, or when OnStar needs to conduct research or troubleshooting, it is delivering enhanced services, it is protecting its rights or the safety of the owner or others, or it is required to by law. *Id.*

[4] Adam Koppel, Note, *Warranting a Warrant: Fourth Amendment Concerns Raised by Law Enforcement's Warrantless Use of GPS and Cellular Tracking*, 64 U. Miami L. Rev. 1061, 1064 (2010).

[5] Joyce Priddy, *Different Uses of GPS Devices*, associatedcontent.com, (September 22, 2007), http://www.associatedcontent.com/article/389315/different_uses_of_gps_devices.html?cat=15; *see also* the Global Positioning System, Recreation, http://www.gps.gov/applications/recreation.

[6] The Global Positioning System, Timing, http://www.gps.gov/applications/timing.

[7] The Global Positioning System, Surveying & Mapping, http://www.gps.gov/applications/survey.

[8] The Global Positioning System, Aviation, http://www.gps.gov/applications/aviation.

[9] Koppel, *supra* note 4, at 1064 (providing statistics on the growing trends in GPS technology).

[10] The Global Positioning System, Public Safety & Disaster Relief, http://www.gps.gov/applications/safety.

[11] To illustrate the government's growing use of GPS technology in the area of criminal investigation, consider that "[i]n response to a Freedom of Information Act request, police in one Virginia locality reported that they used GPS devices in nearly 160 cases from 2005 to 2007." *Id.*

[12] Ben Hubbard, *Police Turn to Secret Weapon: GPS Device*, Wash. Post, A1 (August 13, 2008), available at http://www.washingtonpost.com/wpdyn/content/article/2008/08/12/AR2008081203275.html?nav=rss_metro/va; *see also* Ramya Shah, *From Beepers to GPS: Can the Fourth Amendment Keep Up with Electronic Tracking Technology?*, 2009 U. Ill. J.L. Tech. & Pol'y 281, 281 (Spring 2009) (providing an example of law enforcement's use of a GPS device to tie a suspect to the murder).

[13] *United States v. Garcia*, 474 F.3d 994, 995 (7th Cir. 2007).

[14] *People v. Weaver*, 909 N.E.2d 1195, 1195-96 (N.Y. 2009).

[15] Hutchins, *supra* note 1, at 418-19. The darts consist of a miniaturized GPS receiver, radio transmitter, and battery embedded in a sticky compound material.

[16] *Id.* at 419-20 (internal citations omitted).

[17] *Id.* at 419. Title III of the Omnibus Crime Control and Safe Streets Act of 1958 (P.L. 90-351) regulates the interception of wire, oral, and electronic communications. As such, it does not regulate the use of GPS technology affixed to vehicles and is beyond the scope of this report. For a discussion of wiretapping or electronic eavesdropping, refer to CRS Report 98-326, *Privacy: An Overview of Federal Statutes Governing Wiretapping and Electronic Eavesdropping*, by Gina Stevens and Charles Doyle.

[18] Michael Isikoff, *The Snitch in Your Pocket*, Newsweek (February 19, 2010), http://www.newsweek.com/2010/02/18/the-snitch-in-your-pocket.html.

[19] *Id.*

[20] Almost 50 years ago, in *Lopez v. United States*, 373 U.S. 427, 442 (1963), Chief Justice Warren remarked:

> That the fantastic advances in the field of electronic communication constitute a great danger to the privacy of an individual; that indiscriminate use of such devices in law enforcement raises grave constitutional questions under the Fourth and Fifth Amendment;..."

[21] *See, e.g.*, Hutchins, *supra* note 1, at 464-65; Koppel, *supra* note 4, at 1089; *Maynard*, 615 F.3d at 564; *Weaver*,909 N.E.2d at 1201-02; Kip F. Wainscott, *Unwarranted Intrusion: GPS and the Fourth Amendment*, ACSblog (May 19, 2009, 11:52 AM), http://acslaw.org/node/13444?gclid=CLD254CK56QCFeFM5QodvBbU2A.

[22] *See, e.g.*, *Pineda-Moreno*, 591 F.3d at 1214-16; Tarik N. Jallad, Recent Development, *Old Answers to New Questions: GPS Surveillance and the Unwarranted Need for Warrants*, 11 N.C. J. L. & Tech. 351, 374-75 (Spring 2010); Orin Kerr, Does the Fourth Amendment Prohibit Warrantless GPS Surveillance?, The Volokh Conspiracy (Dec. 13, 2009), http://volokh.com/2009/12/13/does-the-fourth-amendment-prohibit-warrantless-gps-surveillance/.

[23] "The right of the people to be secure in their persons, houses, papers, and effects, against unreasonable searches and seizures, shall not be violated, and no Warrants shall issue, but upon probable cause, supported by Oath or affirmation, and particularly describing the place to be searched, and the persons or things to be seized." U.S. Const. amend. IV.

[24] This protection even includes searches and seizures conducted "beyond the sphere of criminal investigations." *City of Ontario v. Quon*, 130 S.Ct. 2619, 2627 (2010).

[25] Although the Fourth Amendment, like the Fifth Amendment, was originally understood to apply only to federal government action, *see Barron v. City of Baltimore*, 32 U.S. 243, 247-51 (1833), the Supreme Court later found that it became applicable to the states through the Due Process Clause of the Fourteenth Amendment. *Mapp v. Ohio*, 367 U.S.643, 660 (1961).

[26] Garcia, 474 F.3d at 996.

[27] *See, e.g., City of Ontario*, 130 S.Ct. at 2630; *Brigham City v. Stuart*, 547 U.S. 398, 403 (2006); *Groh v. Ramirez*, 540 U.S. 551, 559 (2004); *United States v. Ross*, 456 U.S. 798, 824-25 (1982); *Mincey v. Arizona*, 437 U.S. 385, 390 (1978); *Katz v. United States*, 389 U.S. 347, 357 (1967). The Court has gone back and forth on whether warrantless searches or seizures are presumptively unreasonable or per se unreasonable. It is unclear which approach the Court currently follows.

[28] *Brigham City*, 547 U.S. at 403. As the Court in *Brigham City* outlined, some of these exceptions include law enforcement's engaging "in hot pursuit of a fleeing suspect," preventing "the imminent destruction of evidence," extinguishing a fire on private property and investigating its cause, or assisting "persons who are seriously injured or threatened with such injury." *Id.* (internal quotations and citations omitted).

[29] *See, e.g., Boyd v. United States*, 116 U.S. 616, 627 (1886); *Adams v. New York*, 192 U.S. 585, 598 (1904); *Olmstead v. United States*, 277 U.S. 438, 464-66 (1928); *Goldman v. United States*, 316 U.S. 129, 134-36 (1942); *see also Kyllo v. United States*, 533 U.S. 27, 31-33 (2001) (discussing the historical evolving emphasis of Fourth Amendment protection).

[30] *See, e.g., Silverthorne Lumber Co. v. United States*, 251 U.S. 385 (1920); *Jones v. United States*, 362 U.S. 257, 266 (1960), *overruled on other grounds by United States v. Salvucci*, 448 U.S. 83 (1980); *Silverman v. United States*, 365 U.S. 505, 511-12 (1961); *Warden v. Hayden*, 387 U.S. 294, 304 (1967); *Rakas v. Illinois*, 439 U.S. 128, 143 (1986).

[31] *Warden*, 387 U.S. at 304-05 (discussing the shift of emphasis from property to privacy).

[32] *Katz*, 389 U.S. at 353. This focus finds support in the Amendment's text, which begins by stating that it protects"[t]he right of the people." U.S. Const. amend. IV.

[33] 389 U.S. 347 (1967).

[34] *Kyllo*, 533 U.S. at 33 (quoting *Katz*, 389 U.S. at 353).

[35] The Fourth Amendment's mandates are enforced through the application of an exclusionary rule which generally states that evidence illegally seized may not be used against the defendant. *See, Weeks v. United States*, 232 U.S. 383 (1914) (holding that the Fourth Amendment barred the use of evidence secured through a warrantless search); *Mapp v.Ohio*, 367 U.S. 643 (1961) (holding that the exclusionary rule applies to the states).

[36] *Kyllo*, 533 U.S. at 32. "A search," the Court has explained, "comprises the individual interest in privacy; a seizure deprives the individual of dominion over his or her [person or] personal property." *Horton v. California*, 496 U.S. 128,133 (1990). The use of a GPS to conduct surveillance would seem to fall under the rubric of a search; the attachment ofa GPS device lends itself more to the concept of a seizure. *See United States v. Karo*, 468 U.S. 705, 712-13 (1984)(recognizing the difference in issues raised by the two concepts).

[37] *California v. Greenwood*, 486 U.S. 35, 40-41 (1988).

[38] *United States v. Ciraolo*, 476 U.S. 207, 211 (1986) (quoting *Katz v. United States*, 389 U.S. 347, 360 (1967) (Harlan, J., concurring)); see also Kyllo, 533 U.S. at 33-34.

[39] *Ciraolo*, 476 U.S. at 211; *see also Kyllo*, 533 U.S. at 34.

[40] 533 U.S. 27, 34 (2001).

[41] 476 U.S. 207, 213-15 (1986).

[42] 460 U.S. 276, 281-84 (1983).

[43] However, the Court found that the arrest warrant was valid, as it was based on an affidavit, which contained a significant amount of evidence from sources other than the beeper.

[44] 468 U.S. 705, 713-16 (1984).

[45] *But see*, 468 U.S. at 729-30 (Stevens, J., dissenting) (stating that the beeper's attachment constituted a "seizure.").

[46] The Court declined to decide whether a search warrant to monitor a beeper would require probable cause or reasonable suspicion.

[47] *United States v. Maynard*, 615 F.3d 544, 564 (D.C. Cir. 2010)(listing several states and the relevant legislation in each). *See, e.g.*, Utah Code Ann. §§ 77-23a-4, 77-23a-7, 77-23a-15.5; Minn. Stat. §§ 626A.37, 626A.35; Fla. Stat. §§ 934.06, 934.42; S.C.Code Ann. § 17-30-140; Okla. Stat., tit. 13, §§ 176.6, 177.6; Haw. Rev. Stat. §§ 803-42, 803-44.7; 18 Pa. Cons.Stat. § 5761.

[48] *See State v. Weaver*, 909 N.E.2d 1195 (N.Y. 2009) (GPS use, under state constitution, is unconstitutional without a warrant); *State v. Jackson*, 76 P.3d 217 (Wash. 2003); *State v. Campbell*, 759 P.2d 1040 (Or. 1988); *Delaware v. Biddle*, No. CRIM.A. 05-01-1052, 2005 WL 3073593, at *1 (Del. Com. Pl. May 5, 2005); *see also Commonwealth v. Connolly*, 913 N.E.2d 356 (Mass. 2009) (installation of a GPS device was a seizure).

[49] 909 N.E.2d 1195 (N.Y. 2009).

[50] *Id.* at 1202.

[51] *Id.*

[52] *See Osburn v. State*, 44 P.3d 523 (Nev. 2002); *Foltz v. Commonwealth*, 698 S.E.2d 281 (Va. Ct. App. 2010), *reh'g en banc granted and mandate stayed by* 699 S.E. 2d 522 (Va. Ct. App. 2010).

[53] 698 S.E.3d 281 (Va. Ct. App. 2010), *reh'g en banc granted and mandate stayed by* 699 S.E. 2d 522 (Va. Ct. App.2010).

[54] *Id.* at 286.

[55] *See, e.g.*, *United States v. Garcia*, 474 F.3d 994 (7th Cir. 2007); *United States v. Marquez*, 605 F.3d 604 (8th Cir. 2010); *United States v. Pineda-Moreno*, 591 F.3d 1212 (9th Cir. 2010); *United States v. Eberle*, 993 F.Supp. 794 (D. Mont. 1998); *United States v. Moran*, 349 F. Supp. 2d 425 (N.D.N.Y.2005); *United States v. Burton*, 698 F. Supp. 2d 1303 (N.D. Fl. 2010); *United States v. Williams*, 650 F. Supp. 2d 633 (W.D. KY. 2009); *United States v. Jesus-Nunez*, No. 1:10-CR-00017-01, 2010 WL 2991229, at *1 (July 27, 2010).

[56] 591 F.3d 1212 (9th Cir. 2010).

[57] *Id.* at 1213.

[58] *Id.*

[59] *Id.* at 1214.

[60] *Id.* at 1214-15.

[61] *Id.* at 1216.

[62] *Id.* at 1216-17 (quoting *Knotts*, 460 U.S. at 284) (alterations in original).

[63] *Knotts*, 460 U.S. at 284.

[64] *Pineda-Moreno*, 591 F.3d at 1216 n.2 (quoting *Garcia*, 474 F.3d at 998).

[65] *United States v. Maynard*, 615 F.3d 544 (D.C. Cir. 2010). This was a consolidated case with two defendants, Jones and Maynard. The D.C. Circuit Court of Appeals reversed Jones's conviction but affirmed Maynard's. The government appealed Jones's reversal. As such, the case before the Supreme Court is *United States v. Jones*.

[66] *Id.*

[67] *Id.* at 558.

[68] *Id.* at 567.

[69] *Id.* at 556-58 ("In short, *Knotts* held only that '[a] person traveling in an automobile on public thoroughfares has no reasonable expectation of privacy in his movements from one place to another,' not that such a person has no reasonable expectation of privacy in his movements whatsoever, world without end.").

[70] *Id.* at 558-67.

[71] The D.C. Circuit Court of Appeals reversed Jones's conviction but affirmed Maynard's. The government appealed Jones's reversal. As such, the case before the Supreme Court is *United States v. Jones*, 131 S.Ct. 3064 (2011).

[72] *See, e.g.*, *Connolly*, 913 N.E.2d at 822.

[73] This approach could be called the "Mosaic Theory." The idea is that when GPS surveillance is prolonged, the sum of otherwise publicly exposed activities reveals patterns that are reasonably expected to be private, thus constituting a search, which requires a warrant. *See* Orin Kerr, *D.C. Circuit Introduces "Mosaic Theory" of Fourth Amendment, Holds GPS Monitoring a Fourth Amendment Search*, The Volokh Conspiracy (August 6, 2010), http://volokh.com/2010/08/06/d-c-circuit-introduces-mosaic-theory-of-fourth-amendment-holds-gps-monitoring-a-fourth-amendment-search/. The court in *Maynard* used this theory and tied it to the Supreme Court's dragnet reservation in *Knotts*. However, unlike the 9th and 7th Circuits, the D.C. Circuit read it to apply when law enforcement engages in prolonged surveillance, not just mass surveillance. *Maynard*, 615 F.3d at 557-63.

[74] The United States petitioned for a rehearing *en banc* to the court's decision in *Maynard*. Orin Kerr, *DOJ Petitions for Rehearing in DC Circuit "Mosaic Theory" GPS Surveillance Case*, The Volokh Conspiracy (September 22, 2010), http://volokh.com/2010/09/22/doj-petitions-for-rehearing-in-dc-circuit-mosaic-theory-gps-surveillance-case/.

[75] Orin S. Kerr, *The Fourth Amendment and New Technologies: Constitutional Myths and the Case for Caution*, 102 Mich. L. Rev. 801, 806 (2004).

[76] *See generally* Hutchins, supra note 1; *see also* Renee McDonald Hutchins, *The Anatomy of a Search: Intrusiveness and the Fourth Amendment*, 44 U. Rich. L. Rev. 1185, 1189 n.22 (May 2010) (noting the current debate between whether the legislature or the judiciary is the preferred arbiter in the area of GPS technology).

[77] *Pineda-Moreno*, 591 F.3d at 1216 (quoting *Knotts*, 460 U.S. at 284).

[78] *Weaver*, 909 N.E.2d at 1199.

[79] *Knotts*, 460 U.S. at 284.

[80] Some cite, for example, an Historical Review of the Constitution and Government of Pennsylvania, title page (1759) (Arno Press reprint 1972) (stating that "[t]hose who would give up essential Liberty, to purchase a little temporary Safety, deserve neither Liberty nor Safety") (commonly attributed to Benjamin Franklin).

[81] *Weaver*, 909 N.E. 2d at 1198-99.

[82] *Id.*

[83] *Id.*

[84] Michael Isikoff, *The Snitch in Your Pocket*, Newsweek, February 19, 2010, available at http://www.newsweek.com/ 2010/02/18/the-snitch-in-your-pocket.html; *see also Pineda-Moreno*, 617 F.3d 1120, 1121, 1126 (9th Cir. 2010) (Kozinski, C.J., dissenting from the denial of rehearing en banc).

[85] *Maynard*, 615 F.3d at 558.

[86] *Weaver*, 909 N.E 2d at 1195.

[87] "[O]fficers in Utah can get electronic warrants in about 20 minutes. 'It's not that hard,'" a Utah County Sherriff stated. Janice Peterson, *Conflicting views on no-warrant GPS ruling*, Daily Herald (September 5, 2010), available at http://www.heraldextra.com/news/local/article_6d44220a-e8d1-5d0b-a072-bce72e97a835.html.

In: Legalities of GPS and Cell Phone Surveillance ISBN: 978-1-62257-026-3
Editors: E. Johnson and M. Rodriguez

Chapter 2

GOVERNMENTAL TRACKING OF CELL PHONES AND VEHICLES: THE CONFLUENCE OF PRIVACY, TECHNOLOGY, AND LAW*

Richard M. Thompson

SUMMARY

Technology has advanced considerably since the framers established the constitutional parameters for searches and seizures in the Fourth Amendment. What were ink quills and parchment are now cell phones and the Internet. It is undeniable that these advances in technology threaten to diminish privacy. Law enforcement's use of cell phones and GPS devices to track an individual's movements brings into sharp relief the challenge of reconciling technology, privacy, and law.

Beyond the Constitution, a miscellany of statutes and cases may apply to these tracking activities. One such statute is the Electronic Communications Privacy Act of 1986 (ECPA), P.L. 99-508, 100 Stat. 1848 (1986), which protects individual privacy and governs the methods by which law enforcement may retrieve electronic communications information for investigative purposes, including pen registers, trap and trace devices,

* This is an edited, reformatted and augmented version of the Congressional Research Service Publication, CRS Report for Congress R42109, dated December 1, 2011.

wiretaps, and tracking devices. The primary debate surrounding cell phone and GPS tracking is not whether they are permitted by statute but rather what legal standard should apply: probable cause, reasonable suspicion, or something less.

Legislation has been introduced in the 112th Congress that proposes to update, clarify, or, in some instances, strengthen the privacy interests protected under the law and give law enforcement a clearer framework for obtaining crucial crime-fighting information. In particular, Senator Ron Wyden and Representative Jason Chaffetz introduced identical legislation, S. 1212 and H.R. 2168, entitled the Geolocational Privacy and Surveillance Act, or GPS bill, which would make it unlawful for a service provider to disclose or law enforcement to intercept or use a person's location unless they obtained a warrant based upon probable cause or one of the limited exceptions applies. Senator Patrick J. Leahy has introduced the Electronic Communications Privacy Act Amendment Act of 2011 (S. 1011), which not only includes a warrant requirement for geolocation information, but also overhauls and updates other provisions of federal electronic surveillance law.

Congress is not the only branch confronting this tension between technology and privacy—the Supreme Court has granted certiorari in *United States v. Jones*, 131 S. Ct. 3064 (2011), to determine whether the Fourth Amendment's protection against unreasonable searches and seizures precludes the police from placing a GPS device on a person's vehicle without a warrant. Though the Court has dealt with similar issues in *United States v. Knotts*, 460 U.S. 276 (1983), and *United States v. Karo*, 468 U.S. 705 (1984), in *Jones*, the Court has been asked to determine what effect the prolonged, warrantless use of a tracking device has on a person's privacy interest.

This report will briefly survey Fourth Amendment law as it pertains to the government's tracking programs. It will then summarize federal electronic surveillance statutes and the case law surrounding cell phone location tracking. Next, the report will describe the GPS-vehicle tracking cases and review the pending Supreme Court GPS tracking case, *United States v. Jones*. Finally, the report will summarize the geolocation and electronic surveillance legislation introduced in the 112th Congress.

INTRODUCTION

Technology has advanced considerably since the framers established the constitutional parameters for searches and seizures in the Fourth Amendment.

What were ink quills and parchment are now cell phones and the Internet. It is undeniable that these advances in technology threaten to diminish privacy. Law enforcement's use of cell phones and GPS devices to track an individual's movements brings into sharp relief the challenge of reconciling technology, privacy, and law.

A miscellany of statutes and cases may apply to these tracking programs. One such statute is the Electronic Communications Privacy Act of 1986 (ECPA),[1] which protects individual privacy and governs the methods by which law enforcement may retrieve electronic communications for investigative purposes. ECPA addresses various means for conducting these investigations, including pen registers, trap and trace devices, wiretaps, and tracking devices. The primary debate surrounding statutory regulation of cell phone and GPS tracking is not whether they are permitted, but rather what legal standard should apply: probable cause, reasonable suspicion, or something less. More fundamentally, the Constitution sets a floor for permissible tracking practices.

Legislation has been introduced in the 112th Congress that proposes to update, clarify, or, in some instances, strengthen the privacy interests protected under the law and give law enforcement a clearer framework for obtaining crucial crime-fighting information. In particular, Senator Ron Wyden and Representative Jason Chaffetz introduced identical legislation, S. 1212 and H.R. 2168, the Geolocational Privacy and Surveillance Act (GPS bill), which would make it unlawful for a service provider to disclose a person's location unless law enforcement obtained a warrant based upon probable cause or one of the limited exceptions applies. Senator Al Franken has introduced the Location Privacy and Protection Act of 2011 (S. 1223)—similar to the GPS bill, but which applies only to private, not governmental, actors. Senator Patrick J. Leahy has introduced the Electronic Communications Privacy Act Amendment Act of 2011 (S. 1011), which not only includes a warrant requirement for geolocation information, but also overhauls and updates other provisions of federal electronic surveillance law.

Congress is not the only branch confronting this tension between technology and privacy—the Supreme Court has granted certiorari in *United States v. Jones*, to determine whether the Fourth Amendment's protection against unreasonable searches and seizures precludes the police from placing a GPS device on a person's vehicle without a warrant.[2] Though the Court has dealt with similar issues in *United States v. Knotts*,[3] and *United States v. Karo*,[4] in *Jones*, the Court has been asked to determine what effect the prolonged, warrantless use of a tracking device has on a person's privacy interest.

The use of geolocation information by private actors (e.g., telecommunication companies, commercial service providers) also raises significant privacy concerns.[5] As more computing moves to the "cloud," concerns are raised as to what privacy protections consumers should be accorded. The proposed legislation from the 112th Congress just described applies to both government and private actors, and attempts to address some of these issues. However, an analysis of the private use of this type of information is beyond the scope of this report.

This report will briefly survey Fourth Amendment law as it pertains to the government's tracking programs. It will then summarize federal electronic surveillance statutes and the case law surrounding cell phone location tracking. Next, the report will describe the GPS-vehicle tracking cases and review the Supreme Court GPS tracking case, *United States v. Jones*. Finally, the report will summarize the geolocation and electronic surveillance legislation introduced in the 112th Congress.

FOURTH AMENDMENT AND PRIVACY

The fountainhead of privacy in the United States is the Fourth Amendment, which ensures that "[t]he right of the people to be secure in their persons, houses, papers, and effects, against unreasonable searches and seizures, shall not be violated...."[6] For at least the past 50 years, this provision has been subject to more litigation than any other in the Bill of Rights.[7] This may come as no surprise, considering the Fourth Amendment protects, as Justice Brandeis put it, "the right to be let alone—the most comprehensive of rights and the right most valued by civilized men."[8]

A recurrent theme flows through Fourth Amendment cases: criminals devise new ways to commit crimes and evade the police; the police devise new ways to intercept communications and detect criminal conduct; and the courts are left to sort out the constitutional from the not in these new contexts. In 1928, for example, when police eavesdropped on the telephone conversations of Roy Olmstead and his bootlegging conspirators, the Court refused to label this a violation of the Constitution because the police had not physically trespassed on the defendants' properties in making the wiretaps.[9] The Fourth Amendment protected a person's property interest, the Court held, not abstract things like his own voice.[10] Also, the channel of communication, the telephone wires, extended beyond the defendant's home to the "whole world"—well beyond Olmstead's property interest.[11]

Almost 40 years later the Court changed course, radically altering the constitutional contours of protected privacy by determining that "the Fourth Amendment protects people, not places."[12] In *Katz v. United States*, the FBI eavesdropped on Katz's conversation with an electronic device after he had closed himself inside of a telephone booth. The Court found that act of closing himself in a booth indicated Katz's desire for privacy, and that the FBI had overstepped its bounds when it listened to the contents of Katz's conversation.[13] The Court developed a new standard—the reasonable expectation of privacy—to determine whether an act by the government constitutes a search, thereby triggering a Fourth Amendment analysis. If a person has "exhibited an actual (subjective) expectation of privacy" and it is one "that society is prepared to recognize as 'reasonable,'"[14] then a search in the constitutional sense has occurred, and the court will subject it to further analysis—usually, determining whether there was a warrant or whether an exception to the warrant requirement applies. If, on the other hand, there was no reasonable expectation of privacy, a warrantless search does not offend the Fourth Amendment.

Although *Katz* established that the contents of a conversation are accorded constitutional protection, the Court did not extend this protection to information generated in making the communication. This issue arose in *Smith v. Maryland*, in which the Court held that a person does not have a reasonable expectation of privacy in the telephone numbers he dials.[15] Michael Lee Smith was a thief who robbed a young woman and then harassed her with obscene phone calls. The police used a pen register (without a warrant) to record the numbers dialed from Smith's office. Based on the numbers he dialed, the police determined that Smith was calling the young woman and later arrested him. In concluding that a search had not occurred, the Court reiterated that a person has no legitimate expectation of privacy in information voluntarily given to third parties—in this case, dialed numbers to the phone carrier.[16]

Generally, the Court has not applied the Fourth Amendment to surveillance conducted in public.[17] Under this theory, the police are permitted to, without a warrant, fly a plane[18] or a helicopter[19] in public airspace over a person's private property to look for illegal activity; photograph commercial property "exposed to visual observation from the air" from a plane that is "lawfully within navigable airspace";[20] and attach a tracking device to a suspect's vehicle to track its movements while in public.[21]

Despite granting police wide latitude for searches occurring in public, the Court remains solicitous of privacy in the home. In *Karo v. United States*, the Court held that monitoring the presence of an item in a private residence through the use of a beeper violated the Fourth Amendment rights of the residents, absent a valid warrant.[22] Likewise, when police, without a warrant, used thermal imaging on Danny Kyllo's home to determine if he was using high-intensity heat lamps (usually an indication of growing marijuana), the Court again protected the sanctity of the home, holding that information on activities within a home derived through sense-enhancing technology outside of it was obtained in violation of the Fourth Amendment.[23]

The Constitution, however, is just one font of legal standards that balance privacy interests with law enforcement needs. The Constitution is a floor, not a ceiling. Federal law (and state constitutions and statutes) can provide more protection than the Constitution requires, but no less. There are several comprehensive federal statutes that regulate the use of electronic surveillance— in some instances Congress has seen fit to provide more protection than the constitutional floor, while in others it has not.

FEDERAL SURVEILLANCE STATUTORY FRAMEWORK

As criminal enterprises harness new technologies to commit crime and evade police detection, the police seek to avail themselves of the same technologies in an effort to effectively investigate and prosecute criminal activities. Over the past several years, law enforcement has used cell phone information obtained through service providers to monitor the movements of suspects. Meanwhile, Congress has drawn and redrawn access standards under electronic communication laws. Still, the debate over the use of cell location information is not "*whether* the government can obtain cell site information. Rather, the issue is the *standard* it must meet before a court will authorize such disclosure."[24]

Electronic Communications Privacy Act (ECPA)

In response to *Katz*,[25] Congress enacted Title III of the Omnibus Crime Control and Safe Streets Act of 1968,[26] which is the core of federal domestic surveillance law. Title III prohibits the unauthorized use of surveillance techniques—for instance, bugging and wiretapping—by public and private actors, but permits law enforcement to use such techniques in controlled and well-defined circumstances.[27] In 1986, Congress enacted the Electronic Communications Privacy Act,[28] which amended Title III, to prevent the "unauthorized interception of electronic communications" and "update and clarify Federal privacy protections and standards in light of dramatic changes in new computer and telecommunications technologies."[29] Congress sought to balance the interests of law enforcement with the interest of citizen privacy.[30] There are three main titles in ECPA: the Wiretap Act,[31] the Stored Communications Act,[32] and the Pen Register/Trap Trace Statute.[33]

The first title of ECPA amended Title III of the 1968 Omnibus Crime Control Act, the Wiretap Act, to cover not only wire and oral communications, as originally enacted, but also "electronic communications."[34] Under §2518, the government may obtain a wiretap order and listen to the content of the calls (the words spoken) to and from a suspect only by demonstrating (1) probable cause to believe that a crime was or is being committed; (2) the communication is relevant to that crime; (3) normal investigative procedures have been tried but have failed; and (4) police believe the location from which the communication is made is connected to the crime.[35]

The Pen Register/Trap Trace Statute is found in the second title of ECPA. A "pen register"[36] records numbers dialed from a phone, and a "trap and trace device" captures the telephone number of an incoming call.[37] The pen register and trap-trace devices are the preferred investigatory tools of law enforcement due to the modest standard for justifying their use: the government need only show that "the information likely to be obtained by such installation and use is relevant to an ongoing criminal investigation."[38] This standard, which is significantly less than probable cause or reasonable suspicion, stems from the theory that a person has no reasonable expectation of privacy in the phone numbers he dials.[39] Under this statute, the court wields no power of review but merely requires that the certificate be in proper form.[40] Though this standard is less demanding, there are limitations to the information that police may seek with a pen register or trap-trace device: neither instrument may be used "in a manner so as to constitute a 'tracking device'" without first showing probable cause.[41]

The third title of ECPA is the Stored Wire and Electronic Communications and Transactional Records Access Act, more commonly referred to as the Stored Communications Act (SCA). Section 2703 of the SCA prescribes the manner in which service providers may divulge records and *contents* of wire and electronic communications to the government.[42] Under subsections (a) and (b), if the government seeks the contents of a communication that has been in storage less than 180 days, it must obtain a warrant (supported by probable cause) under Rule 41 of the Federal Rules of Criminal Procedure.[43] Under §2703(c), if the government seeks only "a record or other information pertaining to a subscriber,"[44] it can require the service provider to turn over the documents if they "offer[] specific and articulable facts showing that there are reasonable grounds to believe that the contents of a wire or electronic communication, or the records or other information sought, are relevant and material to an ongoing criminal investigation."[45]

The most significant provision of the SCA for purposes of cell location data is the definition of "electronic communication." This definition excludes "any communication from a tracking device,"[46] which is defined as "an electronic or mechanical device which permits the tracking of the movement of a person or object."[47] In the courts that have confronted this issue, much hinges on whether a cell phone should be categorized as a "tracking device."[48]

In 1994, Congress enacted the Communications Assistance for Law Enforcement Act (CALEA), which required communication providers to develop protocols for ensuring law enforcement access to information for which it had lawful authorization.[49] Congress authorized funding for these service providers to assist in upgrading their systems.[50] CALEA required telecommunication carriers to ensure they had the ability to provide law enforcement "access to call-identifying information."[51] It should be noted, however, that the text explicitly excluded location information: "such call-identifying information shall not include any information that may disclose the physical location of the subscriber (except to the extent that the location may be determined from the telephone number)...."[52]

Evidentiary Standards of Proof under ECPA

It is helpful to think of the requisite evidentiary proof required for disclosure of electronic communications as a tiered system, ranging from highest (or most stringent) to lowest (or least stringent).[53] The most stringent is the Wiretap Act standard—the "super-warrant" requirement.[54] Among other conditions, the Wiretap Act requires a detailed affidavit of the facts warranting the search, the specific time and date of the proposed search, and an explanation of why other investigatory methods are insufficient.[55] Next are tracking devices, as defined in 18 U.S.C. §3117, which may require a warrant (based upon probable cause) under Rule 41 of the Rules of Criminal Procedure.[56] Below that falls §2703(d) of the Stored Communications Act, which requires "specific and articulable facts showing that there are reasonable grounds to believe that the contents of a wire or electronic communication, or the records or other information sought, are relevant and material to an ongoing criminal investigation."[57] As discussed below, the courts are split on whether §2703(d) applies to historical records, real-time records, or both. Finally, the lowest tier, contained in the Pen Register/Trap Trace statute, is a certification that the "information likely to be obtained is relevant to an ongoing criminal investigation being conducted by that agency."[58] Police need not present specific facts as the higher tiers require, but merely must present the certification. This requirement has been described by one federal court as a "low one."[59]

The differences in these standards are important, as the debate in state and federal courts over cell location information turns on which tier—or level of proof—the government must prove to obtain the information; some courts require a showing of probable cause, while others permit an order based on "specific and articulable facts."

CELL PHONE SURVEILLANCE IN THE COURTS

Federal electronic surveillance law is a patchwork of terms and standards. Nowhere is this more apparent than in the federal courts' application of ECPA to government requests for cell site location information.[60] Policy arguments exist both for facilitating access and restricting it. The government, on one hand, argues that "cell site information is an important investigatory tool which is used ... to, among other things, help to determine where to establish physical surveillence [sic] and to help locate kidnapping victims, fugitives, and targets of criminal investigations."[61] Privacy proponents, on the other hand, want to ensure "Big Brother stays out of your pocket" and argue that the government is trying to turn the cell phone system into a "vast network for warrantless physical surveillance."[62]

Though these requests for cell site location information have become more frequent in the lower courts, only one circuit has directly confronted the issue of cell location information. The Third Circuit Court of Appeals decided in favor of the government, holding that the "specific and articulable facts" standard of the Stored Communications Act (SCA) was sufficient to obtain cell location information. Many magistrate judges, on the other hand, have rejected this approach, instead requiring probable cause. At times, the outcome in the lower courts has been influenced by whether the government was seeking historical versus prospective cell site information.[63]

Third Circuit Approach

In 2010, the Third Circuit confronted as a matter of first impression a government request for historical cell location information.[64] The government applied for a court order under the Stored Communications Act to compel a cell phone service provider to produce a customer's historical cellular tower data relating to that customer's location.[65] In a lengthy opinion, the magistrate judge had denied this request, concluding that an order of this type, whether historical or real-time, could only be granted upon a showing of probable cause.[66] The District Court, without analysis, affirmed the magistrate judge's opinion.[67] The Third Circuit reversed, holding that the magistrate judges have the discretion whether to require the government to show "specific and articulable facts" under the Stored Communication Act or probable cause under a general warrant theory, depending on whether access to this information under the lower "articulable facts" standard would violate the Fourth Amendment.[68]

Before the lower court, the government primarily contended that a cell phone was not a tracking device and thus cell location information could be obtained under the Stored Communications Act.[69] This proposition was crucial to the government's argument because location information from a "tracking device"[70] cannot be sought under the Stored Communications Act.[71] If this argument failed, the government would be required to show probable cause. A tracking device, the magistrate judge noted, is anything which "permits the tracking of movement of a person or object."[72] She concluded that a cell phone undoubtedly constituted a "tracking device" because it could locate a person to within 50 feet and continuously broadcasted information.[73] She further pointed out that "[b]y virtue of cell phone technology, law enforcement may now electronically monitor our movements with as much—indeed, ofttimes more—scope and precision as by its traditional methods of visual surveillance and/or installation of a 'beeper.'"[74]

Because the cell phone was considered a tracking device, and the Stored Communications Act excludes tracking devices from its reach, the magistrate judge concluded that the Stored Communications Act could not govern this request, and therefore any retrieval of information must be authorized under the normal warrant process as required by Rule 41 of the Federal Rules of Criminal Procedure.[75]

On appeal from the district court, the government narrowed its focus, arguing that historical cell location information (rather than both historical and prospective information) falls within the Stored Communications Act. The

Third Circuit agreed, reversed the lower courts, and held that the Stored Communications Act's intermediate "articulable and specific facts" standard applied.[76] The government's main contention was again that cell phones were not tracking devices, but, further, that the location data was derived not from an "electronic communication,"[77] but from a "wire communication."[78] "'Wire communication' means any aural transfer made in whole or in part through the use of facilities for the transmission of communications by the aid of wire, cable, or other like connection between the point of origin and the point of reception...."[79] The Third Circuit accepted that the historical location information requested was "derived from a 'wire communication' and does not itself comprise a separate 'electronic communication.'"[80] Even if a cell phone was a tracking device excluded from "electronic communication" as described in §2510, it would not matter, as tracking devices are not excluded from the definition of "wire communication."[81] Relying on the phrase "may be issued" in §2703(d), the court concluded that the decision whether to require a warrant or an order under the intermediate standard is discretionary—that is, a court can choose to require either a warrant or a court order based on the lesser standard, depending on the facts.[82]

Conflict in the Lower Courts

Though the other circuit courts have yet to interpret the requests for cell phone location information under the Stored Communications Act, the district courts, and in particular magistrate judges, have written quite lengthy opinions on the issue, and have reached divergent conclusions.

For instance, the Southern District of Texas found unpersuasive the government's stance that the Stored Communications Act applied to its request for prospective or real-time cell location information.[83] The analysis, similar to that employed by the magistrate judge in the Third Circuit case, begins with the definition of tracking device. the government argued that cell location information did not fit the definition of tracking device—"an electronic or mechanical device which permits the tracking of the movement of a person or [object]"[84]—since it did not provide detailed location information. With the advance in cell phone technology, the court found this argument wanting, as tracking was becoming very precise, and further because the definition of tracking device does not differentiate between general and specific vicinity tracking.[85] Holding that a cell phone falls into the definition of "tracking device," the court then analyzed each major section of ECPA—the Pen

Register/Trap Trace Statute, the Wiretap Act, and the Stored Communications Act—to determine if any of the sections apply to cell location information.

The court dismissed this information as obtainable under the Pen Register Statute, noting that Congress explicitly prohibited law enforcement from obtaining any location information under this statute.[86] Next, the court excluded the "super-warrant wiretap standard," as the government was not seeking to obtain the *contents* of the defendant's conversations, but rather the *location* of the caller.[87] Finally, the court eliminated the Stored Communications Act based on the definitions used in that act. First, the SCA must apply to an "electronic communication service." "Electronic communication service," in turn, is defined as "any service which provides to users thereof the ability to send or receive wire or electronic communications."[88] This location information cannot be from an electronic communication, the court concluded, as the definition specifically excludes "tracking devices." It also cannot be a "wire communication" because a wire communication involves the "human voice."[89] Based on this logical sequence of interlocking definitions, the court held that the SCA did not apply, and that the traditional warrant would be necessary.[90]

This analysis by the Southern District of Texas has been followed in a majority of jurisdictions.[91] A minority of courts, on the other hand, have held that the government need not establish probable cause, relying primarily on the hybrid theory.

Hybrid Theory

Under the hybrid theory, the government purports to have authority to obtain prospective cell location information by combining provisions of the Pen Register Statute and the Stored Communications Act.[92] The Pen Register Statute was traditionally used by law enforcement to record the dialed numbers for outgoing calls, and the trap and trace device to record incoming calls.[93] Pen registers are used not only for recording telephone numbers dialed but also to record "signaling information,"[94] language that was expanded by the USA PATRIOT Act in 2001.[95] To get approval under the Pen Register Statute, law enforcement need only show that the material requested is relevant to an ongoing investigation.[96] Although cell location information may fit within this definition of "signaling information," the Communications Assistance for Law Enforcement Act (CALEA) of 1994 prohibits government access to location disclosing information gained "solely pursuant to the authority for pen registers and trap and trace devices ..."[97] Some courts rely on this "solely pursuant" language, or "exception clause," to conclude that the Pen Register/Trap Trace Statute may not be used as the sole means for obtaining cell location information but can be used in conjunction with another statutory mechanism.

The hybrid theory looks to the Stored Communications Act as that other mechanism. Section 2703(c)(1) of the SCA provides that "a governmental entity may require a provider of electronic communication service or remote computing service to disclose a record or other information pertaining to a subscriber to or customer of such service."[98] Cell location information, the theory goes, is information that pertains to a subscriber of cellular phone service.[99] There is, however, a roadblock to this theory: cell location information may appear to derive from an "electronic communication" from a cell phone to a cell tower, but the act excludes any communication from a tracking device from an "electronic communication."

As was shown above, the definition of electronic communication excludes any "communication from a tracking device."[100] Thus it may seem that cell phone tracking information cannot be obtained under this theory. Courts accepting the hybrid theory, however, have pointed out that "information on the location of cell towers is not the 'service' to which a cellular customer subscribes. Instead, the user subscribes to the voice—and perhaps data—transmission capabilities provided by the cellular carrier."[101] By focusing on the type of service the customer subscribes to, and not the nature of the location information being relayed, the hybrid theory overcomes this attack.

There is another hurdle to the hybrid theory: it is argued that the Stored Communications Act was intended to cover only historical, not prospective information.[102] To surmount this limitation, the theory "circles back to the Pen/Trap statute ... [and] asserts that disclosure of cell site location information is authorized by the SCA and can be collected in real time by virtue of the Pen/Trap Statute."[103] With those concerns arguably overcome, the courts rely on §2703(d)'s "specific and articulable facts" standard as controlling these requests.

The Eastern District of New York is not alone in accepting this theory,[104] but most jurisdictions have rejected it.[105] Relying on legislative history, at least one court has noted that CALEA was never intended to expand the reach of existing surveillance law.[106]

A majority of the courts require law enforcement to obtain a warrant to access cell location information. But it should be noted that there has been little appellate case law on cell phone tracking, as there appears to be no incentive for defendants to raise the issue—ECPA does not contain an exclusionary rule to prevent the admission of improperly obtained evidence.[107] Thus far, only the Third Circuit has directly ruled on this issue.

Governmental Surveillance of Vehicles

Like surveillance of cell phone location, the government uses GPS devices to track the location of vehicles.[108] Again, the courts have been asked to reconcile privacy interests and the needs of law enforcement in an age of emerging technology. In contrast to the cell phone tracking cases, the vehicle tracking cases have focused on constitutional and not statutory provisions.

United States v. Knotts: Surveillance on Public Roadways

In *United States v. Knotts*, law enforcement attached a tracking device to a can of chloroform, which was subsequently transported by the defendant in his car to a secluded cabin.[109] The police used the tracking device to learn of his location and then obtained a warrant based on this information.[110] When executing the search at the cabin, the police found a drug laboratory and materials to make illegal drugs.[111] The question presented was whether this monitoring violated the defendant's Fourth Amendment rights. The Supreme Court held that since a "person traveling in an automobile on public thoroughfares has no reasonable expectation of privacy in his movements from one place to another," this type of monitoring did not violate the defendant's Fourth Amendment rights.[112] The Court further stated that "scientific enhancement of this sort raises no constitutional issues which visual surveillance would not raise."[113] According to *Knotts*, if the police could theoretically track a suspect by the naked eye, they can use technology to do the same thing.

United States v. Karo: Surveillance on Private Property

In *United States v. Karo*, the Court confronted the issue of "whether the monitoring of beeper in a private residence, a location not open to visual surveillance, violates the Fourth Amendment rights of those who have a justifiable interest in the privacy of the residence."[114] In *Karo*, Drug

Enforcement Administration (DEA) agents attached a tracking device to a can of ether and tracked the can's movements between multiple private residences and storage facilities.[115] The agents obtained a warrant to search a house rented by one of the defendants based on the information derived from the tracking device.[116] In concluding that use of the tracking device constituted an unreasonable search, the Court first spelled out basic Fourth Amendment principles: "private residences are places in which the individual normally expects privacy free of governmental intrusion not authorized by a warrant, and that expectation is plainly one that society is prepared to recognize as justifiable."[117]

Unlike *Knotts*, the Court refused to accept the idea that the government "should be completely free from the constraints of the Fourth Amendment to determine by means of an electronic device, without a warrant and without probable cause or reasonable suspicion, whether a particular article—or a particular person, for that matter—is in an individual's home at a particular time."[118] This case was distinguishable from *Knotts* because the "information obtained in *Knotts* was 'voluntarily conveyed to anyone who wanted to look.'"[119] This gets back to the idea that information a person voluntarily gives to another person—whether it is one's public location or telephone numbers dialed (think *Smith v. Maryland*)—is no longer private and no longer afforded Fourth Amendment protection.

These two decisions left unresolved several lingering issues. Is the public versus private distinction a bright-line rule? Is prolonged surveillance permissible so long as it could have been done by visual surveillance? Does the use of advanced technology, such as GPS that enhances a police officer's senses, ever affect a Fourth Amendment analysis? The courts of appeals were quickly asked to answer these questions.

GPS Tracking in the Seventh and Ninth Circuits

The Seventh and Ninth Circuits have held that the use of a GPS tracking device is not a search afforded Fourth Amendment protection. In *United States v. Garcia*, Judge Posner analogized GPS surveillance to "cameras mounted on lampposts or satellite imaging,"[120] which are not considered searches. The Seventh Circuit, however, was not confronted with the question as to whether *all* tracking of vehicles on public ways is permissible, as the defendant did not raise this issue on appeal. The court did say that the activity at issue, "namely following a car on a public street, ... is unequivocally *not* a search within the meaning of the amendment."[121]

In *United States v. Pineda-Moreno*, law enforcement entered Pineda-Moreno's property and attached a GPS device to his vehicle while it was parked in his driveway.[122] Pineda-Moreno challenged this monitoring not on the basis that the surveillance's continuity exceeded *Knotts* in scope, but rather that police were not permitted to use technology not in general public use as described in *Kyllo v. United States*.[123] Again, the Ninth Circuit rejected this argument, stating that just because GPS made the police more effective at tracking the suspect does not mean that this new form of tracking is unconstitutional; it refused to "equate efficiency with unconstitutionality...."[124]

United States v. Jones: Supreme Court Review

The Supreme Court confronts the issue of government tracking once again in *United States v. Jones*.[125] Using an expired warrant, an FBI task force attached a GPS tracking device to Jones's Jeep Grand Cherokee while it was parked in a public lot in Maryland.[126] For four weeks, the government tracked the movements of Jones's car with an accuracy to within 50-100 feet.[127]

Based on this surveillance, the government retrieved over 2,000 pages of GPS data and was able to track Jones to a stash house in Maryland where it ultimately found large amounts of cocaine.[128] Prior to his trial, Jones filed a motion to suppress this evidence, which was denied except for evidence obtained while his vehicle was parked in his garage.[129]

Jones appealed the constitutionality of both the installation and the subsequent surveillance of his movements. The D.C. Circuit Court of Appeals did not address the installation issue, but instead reversed on the basis that a prolonged, 24-hour surveillance without a warrant was a search, and thus violated Jones's Fourth Amendment right to privacy.[130] The government argued this case was on all fours with *Knotts*—that a "person traveling in an automobile on public thoroughfares has no reasonable expectation of privacy in his movements from one place to another."[131] Jones argued that the use of a GPS is much more pervasive than the beeper used in *Knotts*, and that society is likely to recognize an expectation of privacy in the "pattern, or sum total, of an individual's daily activities."[132] The D.C. Circuit, accepting Jones's argument, relied on Justice Rehnquist's dicta in *Knotts* that further Court oversight could be triggered under different circumstances: "if [a] dragnet-type law enforcement practice[] as respondent envisions should eventually occur, there will be time enough then to determine whether different constitutional principles may be applicable."[133] Ultimately, the D.C. Circuit held that "[s]ociety recognizes Jones's expectation of privacy in his movements over the course of a month as reasonable, and the use of the GPS device to monitor those movements defeated that reasonable expectation."[134]

The Supreme Court has granted certiorari in *Jones* based upon two distinct questions: (1)"Whether the warrantless use of a tracking device on respondent's vehicle to monitor its movements on public streets violated the Fourth Amendment"; and (2) "Whether the government violated respondent's Fourth Amendment rights by installing the GPS tracking device on his vehicle without a valid warrant and without his consent."[135]

As to the first question, much of the debate swirls around Justice Rehnquist's dragnet passage in *Knotts*, and whether he was referring to a program of mass surveillance of the public or prolonged surveillance of a single person.[136] In its brief, the government notes that the Court has used the term "dragnet" to refer to "mass or widespread searches or seizures that are conducted without individualized suspicion," and should not be applied to surveillance of a single individual.[137] Jones counters by noting that "'dragnet' can refer to 'any system for catching a person, esp. a fugitive.'"[138] This dragnet theory should not be limited solely to mass surveillance, Jones argues, but should cover prolonged, warrantless surveillance of one person. This question also implicates the public-private dichotomy and whether use of sensory-enhancing technology can turn an otherwise constitutionally permitted investigation into an unconstitutional search. The government argues that the use of technology to collect information in public "does not make the information any less public."[139] Based on that assumption, *Knotts* would apply and the GPS surveillance would not be a search. Jones argues, to the contrary, that the government can obtain information through GPS surveillance to a degree not feasible through visual surveillance. This pattern information is more intrusive than a general search, thus interfering with an individual's reasonable expectation of privacy.

As to the second question, the D.C. Circuit did not reach the issue of whether the installation of the GPS device on Jones's Jeep was in and of itself a Fourth Amendment violation. The Ninth Circuit has held that attachment of a GPS device on a vehicle while parked in the suspect's driveway was not a Fourth Amendment violation, as the car was parked in an area open to public view and the suspect had not exhibited an expectation of privacy in the undercarriage of his car.[140] Using similar reasoning, the Fifth Circuit held that the government's attachment of a GPS device to a car in a public place did not violate the suspect's Fourth Amendment rights, as the car was parked in plain view and the monitoring did not intrude on the suspect's privacy.[141] The First Circuit, on the other hand, held that attaching a tracking device on a vehicle in a public parking lot violates the Fourth Amendment.[142]

PENDING LEGISLATION BEFORE THE 112TH CONGRESS

Several bills have been introduced in the 112th Congress to amend federal surveillance laws.[143] A broad coalition of industry and privacy advocates including Apple, Google, AT&T, the American Civil Liberties Union, and the Constitution Project—dubbed the Digital Due Process Coalition— has joined to advocate for the passage of these measures.[144] The Department of Justice also advocates a clarification of existing surveillance law, but supports a lower standard that would impose a lesser burden on law enforcement.[145]

Electronic Communications Privacy Act Amendments Act of 2011 (S. 1011)

On May 17, 2011, Senate Judiciary Chairman Patrick Leahy introduced legislation to update federal surveillance law, with a focus on protecting consumer privacy.[146] The Electronic Communications Privacy Act Amendments Act of 2011 (S. 1011) would amend numerous provisions of ECPA, including the Stored Communications Act.[147]

Section 5 would prohibit the government from accessing or using a device to acquire geolocation information, unless the government obtains a warrant based upon probable cause or a court order under Title I or Title IV of the Foreign Intelligence Surveillance Act (FISA) of 1978. There are two exceptions to this requirement for court authorization: (1) to respond to an emergency call by the user of the device; and (2) if the owner of the device gives express consent.

In an emergency, law enforcement may acquire geolocation information if it is determined that an emergency situation exists that (1) involves immediate danger of death or serious bodily injury to another person, conspiratorial activities characteristic of organized crime, or an immediate threat to national security; (2) requires the accessing of geolocation before a court order could be obtained; and (3) there are adequate grounds upon which a court order could be obtained. If law enforcement accesses information based on this emergency exception, it must then apply for a warrant within 48 hours of accessing the information. If a warrant is not obtained, this activity must terminate immediately. If evidence is obtained in violation of this law, an exclusionary clause will apply, which requires that this evidence not be admitted at trial.

Providers of electronic communication services, remote computing service, or geolocation information service would be required to assist law enforcement with accessing the geolocation information permitted under a lawfully obtained warrant. The service providers would in turn be compensated for reasonable expenses incurred in providing such information. Providers are also given immunity from suit for releasing information to the government pursuant to a request under this act.

Section 6 would prohibit the government from requesting contemporaneous or prospective geolocation information from a service provider unless the government met the same warrant standards—that is, obtained a warrant under Rule 41 of the Federal Rules of Criminal Procedure. This act, however, would allow law enforcement to access historical geolocation information based upon a proof of "specific and articulable facts," the same standard contained in the Stored Communications Act.

The bill also permits law enforcement to retrieve general information about the target of the search on a lesser showing, including the name and address of the subscriber, the times and durations of calls, and the means and source of payment, but expressly excluding location information. Currently, the law permits access to a "record or other information pertaining to a subscriber...."[148] S. 1011 specifies which records could be accessed by law enforcement.

Geolocational Privacy and Surveillance Act (GPS Bill; S. 1212 and H.R. 2168)

On June 15, 2011, Senator Ron Wyden and Representative Jason Chaffetz introduced companion bills, the Geolocational Privacy and Surveillance Act, or GPS bill.[149] The GPS bill would clarify and establish the standards the government must meet to monitor an individual's movements.

Under the GPS bill, law enforcement's sole means for acquiring geolocation information would be pursuant to a warrant under Rule 41 of the Federal Rules of Criminal Procedure or the Foreign Intelligence Surveillance Act (FISA) of 1978.[150] It would appear that the Stored Communications Act or the Pen Register/Trap and Trace Act would no longer be mechanisms for acquiring this information.

The bill contains a broad prohibition against the disclosure or use of geolocation information.[151] Specifically, it makes it unlawful for any person[152] to (A) intentionally intercept geolocation information pertaining to another person; (B) intentionally disclose geolocation information pertaining to another person when it is known that information was obtained in violation of the act; (C) intentionally use any geolocation information knowing that the information was obtained in violation of the act; or (D) intentionally disclose information that was lawfully obtained under the act, but not authorized to be released to third parties.[153]

There are several exceptions to the prohibition against the use of geolocation information. Providers of geolocation information service[154] may intercept, use, or disclose geolocation information in the normal course of business when it is a "necessary incident to the rendition of service or to the protection of the rights or property of the provider of that service." The service providers, however, shall not randomly monitor customers except to service their systems.

There is also an exception for surveillance conducted for national security purposes. Any agent or officer of the United States is permitted to conduct surveillance as authorized under the Foreign Intelligence Surveillance Act of 1978.

There are two consent provisions in the bill. First, it is not unlawful to intercept geolocation information of a person if that person gives prior consent to such interception. Even if consent is given, however, the information cannot be used for purposes of committing a criminal act in violation of the Constitution or laws of the United States. Second, parents can consent to law enforcement use of the information if a child becomes missing.

In cases of emergency, law enforcement or emergency responders are permitted to use geolocation information to respond to a person requesting assistance (i.e., a 911 call).[155] Also, the police may use this information "in circumstances in which it is reasonable to believe that the life or safety of the person is threatened, to assist the person." If a phone is stolen or taken by fraud, police are permitted to use geolocation information to locate the phone so long as the owner of the phone consents to such use.

Police may use geolocation information if they obtain a warrant in accordance with Federal Rule of Criminal Procedure 41 or as otherwise permitted under the Foreign Intelligence Surveillance Act of 1978. This would codify the practice of federal courts that are currently requiring a warrant based upon probable cause to obtain geolocation information, and would require courts that instead have been relying on the Stored Communications Act's standard of "specific and articulable facts" to follow the majority warrant approach. To permit this change, the act would amend Rule 41 to include geolocation information in the list of items subject to the warrant requirement.

The United States Attorney General and the states' Attorneys General are permitted to intercept geolocation information without a warrant if they (1) reasonably believe that an emergency situation exists, which can include an immediate danger of death or serious physical injury to any person, conspiratorial activities threatening the national security interest, and conspiratorial activities characteristic of organized crime; (2) there are grounds in which an order could be entered to authorize such interception; and (3) an application is then requested within 48 hours after the interception occurs.

The GPS bill contains an exclusionary rule, meaning no evidence acquired in violation of the act may be received in evidence in any trial or other judicial proceeding. This is different from ECPA, which does not contain an exclusionary rule. In addition to this exclusionary remedy, any person whose geolocation information is intercepted may seek civil remedies. The person may seek equitable remedies, damages (money), and reasonable attorneys fees and litigation costs. The damages would be the greatest of (1) whatever the actual damages are to the injured party, and any profits the violator may have made from the violation; (2) $100 a day for each day the entity is in violation of the act; or (3) $10,000. There is a complete defense, however, against any civil and criminal liability if the person believed in good faith that his interception or use of a person's geolocation was permitted under this act. There is also a two-year statute of limitation for such claims. If it is determined that a person willfully or deliberately violated the act, the government is permitted to take disciplinary action against him.

Section 4 of the GPS bill would amend 18 U.S.C. §1309(h), which criminalizes fraudulently obtaining a person's phone records, to include geolocation information to the types of records subject to this law. Within 180 days after enactment of this act, the United States Sentencing Commission would be required to amend the sentencing guidelines to take into account this revision of §1309.

Conclusion

Congress, the courts, and the people will continue to grapple with "what limits there are upon [the] power of technology to shrink the realm of guaranteed privacy."[156] Some observers believe that ECPA has lived its useful life and should be amended to remain effective. One commentator notes that the "changes in modern technology and shifting security concerns ... result in ambiguous, overlapping guidance in the area of cell phone tracking."[157] Several Members of Congress have introduced legislation to mend this perceived problem, and overhaul the current federal surveillance regime. The Supreme Court has also been asked to weigh in on this debate about the convergence of law and technology in the form of GPS tracking of a person's car. These cases and legislation have the potential to significantly impact the relationship among law, privacy, and technology.

End Notes

[1] Electronic Communications Privacy Act of 1986, P.L. 99-508, 100 Stat. 1848 (codified as amended in scattered sections of 18 U.S.C.).

[2] United States v. Maynard, 615 F.3d 544, 555-56 (D.C. Cir. 2010), *cert. granted sub nom.* United States v. Jones, 131 S. Ct. 3064 (2011) (No. 10-1259) (oral arguments held on November 8, 2011).

[3] United States v. Knotts, 460 U.S. 276 (1983).

[4] United States v. Karo, 468 U.S. 705 (1984).

[5] *See* CRS Report R41756, *Privacy Protections for Personal Information Online*, by Gina Stevens.

[6] U.S. CONST. amend. IV.

[7] 1 WAYNE R. LAFAVE, SEARCH AND SEIZURE: A TREATISE ON THE FOURTH AMENDMENT IX (4th ed. 2004).

[8] Olmstead v. United States, 277 U.S. 438, 478 (1928) (Brandeis, J., dissenting); *see generally* Samuel D. Warren & Louis D. Brandeis, *The Right to Privacy*, 4 HARV. L. REV. 193 (1890). For a general overview of privacy law, see Stevens, *supra* note 5.

[9] *Olmstead*, 277 U.S. at 464-65.

[10] *Id.*

[11] *Id.* at 465.

[12] Katz v. United States, 389 U.S. 347, 351 (1967).

[13] *Id.* at 352-53.

[14] *Id.* at 361 (Harlan, J., concurring).

[15] Smith v. Maryland, 442 U.S. 735, 745-46 (1979).

[16] *Id.* at 742; *see also* United States v. Miller, 425 U.S. 435, 442-43 (1976) (holding that financial statements and deposit slips transmitted to bank were not protected from police inquiry because they had been turned over to a third party).

[17] Ric Simmons, *Why 2007 Is Not Like 1984: A Broader Perspective on Technology's Effect on Privacy and Fourth Amendment Jurisprudence*, 97 J. CRIM. L. & CRIMINOLOGY 531, 549 (2007).

[18] California v. Ciraolo, 476 U.S. 207, 215 (1986) (holding that naked-eye search from airplane at 1,000 feet was not a search).

[19] Florida v. Riley, 488 U.S. 445, 451-52 (1989) (holding that surveillance from helicopter at 400 feet was not a search).

[20] Dow Chem. Co. v. United States, 476 U.S. 227, 238-39 (1986).

[21] United States v. Knotts, 460 U.S. 276, 285 (1983). For a more detailed discussion of this case, see *United States v. Knotts*: Surveillance on Public Roadways, *infra* p. 15.

[22] United States v. Karo, 468 U.S. 705, 718 (1984) (upholding introduction of evidence found during search that was based in part on impermissible beeper monitoring; warrant was independently sustainable by additional information).

[23] Kyllo v. United States, 533 U.S. 27, 34 (2001) (holding that "obtaining by sense-enhancing technology any information regarding the interior of the home that could not otherwise have been obtained without physical intrusion into a constitutionally protected area, constitutes a search—at least where (as here) the technology in question is not in general public use") (citation omitted).

[24] *In re* Application of the United States of America for an Order Authorizing the Disclosure of Prospective Cell Site Information, No. 06-MISC-004, 2006 U.S. Dist. LEXIS 73324, *2 (E.D. Wis. October 6, 2006).

[25] Matthew Minkle Werdegar, *Lost? The Government Knows Where You Are: Cellular Telephone Call Location Technology and the Expectation of Privacy*, 10 STAN. L. & POL'Y REV. 103, 109 (1998).

[26] Omnibus Crime Control and Safe Streets Act of 1968, P.L. 90-351, 82 Stat. 197.

[27] 1 JAMES G. CARR & PATRICIA L. BELLIA, THE LAW OF ELECTRONIC SURVEILLANCE §1.3 (2011).

[28] Electronic Communications Privacy Act of 1986, P.L. 99-508, 100 Stat. 1848 (codified as amended in scattered sections of 18 U.S.C.); *see* CRS Report R41733, *Privacy: An Overview of the Electronic Communications Privacy Act*, by Charles Doyle; *see also* CARR & BELLIA, *supra note* 27, §1.14.

[29] S.Rept. 99-541, at 1 (1986).

[30] *Id.* at 5; H.Rept. 99-647, at 19 (1986).

[31] 18 U.S.C. §§2510-2520 (2006).

[32] 18 U.S.C. §§2701-2712 (2006).

[33] 18 U.S.C. §§3121-3127 (2006).

[34] 18 U.S.C. §§2510-2520.

[35] 18 U.S.C. §2518.

[36] 18 U.S.C. §3127(3) (A "pen register" is defined as "a device or process which records or decodes dialing, routing, addressing, or signaling information transmitted by an instrument or facility from which a wire or electronic communication is transmitted.").

[37] 18 U.S.C. §3127(4) (A "trap and trace device" is defined as "a device or process which captures the incoming electronic or other impulses which identify the originating number or other dialing, routing, addressing, and signaling information reasonably likely to identify the source of a wire or electronic communication, provided, however, that such information shall not include the contents of any communication.").

[38] 18 U.S.C. §3123(a)(1).

[39] Smith v. Maryland, 442 U.S. 735 (1979).

[40] *See In re* Application of the United States of America for an Order: (1) Authorizing the Installation and Use of a Pen Register and Trap and Trace Device; (2) Authorizing the Release of Subscriber and Other Information; and (3) Authorizing the Disclosure of Location-Based Services, Nos. 1:06-MC-6, 1:06-MC-7, 2006 WL 1876847, *2 (N.D. Ind. July 5, 2006).

[41] *In re* Applications of the United States of America for Orders Pursuant to Title 18, United States Code, Section 2703(d) to Disclose Subscriber Information and Historical Cell Site Information for Mobile Identification Numbers: (XXX) XXX-AAAA, (XXX) XXX-BBBB,

and (XXX) XXX-CCCC, 509 F. Supp. 2d 64, 68 (D. Mass. 2007) (citing 47 U.S.C. §1002(a)(2)(B) (2006)).

[42] 18 U.S.C. §§2703, 2702 (2006) ("A person or entity providing electronic communication service to the public shall not knowingly divulge to any person or entity the contents of the communication while in electronic storage by that service."); *see* CARR & BELLIA, *supra note* 27, §1.17.

[43] 18 U.S.C. §2703(a); FED. R. CRIM. P. 41(d).

[44] 18 U.S.C. §2703(c).

[45] 18 U.S.C. §2703(d).

[46] 18 U.S.C. §2711 (2006) (cross-referencing 18 U.S.C. §2510 for definitions); 18 U.S.C. §2510(12)(C).

[47] 18 U.S.C. §3117 (2006).

[48] Title I of ECPA references the use of tracking devices. 18 U.S.C. §3117(b); *see also* FED. R. CRIM. P. 41 ("After receiving an affidavit or other information, a magistrate judge—or if authorized by Rule 41(b), a judge of a state court of record—must issue the warrant if there is probable cause to search for and seize a person or property or to *install and use a tracking device.*") (emphasis added). Congress included §3117 to ensure that mobile tracking devices could be used when a suspect crosses state lines. The Senate report states that this was merely a jurisdictional clarification that was not intended to affect the legal standards required for tracking authorization. S.Rept. 99-541, at 10 (1986). Section 3117 broadly defines "tracking device" as "an electronic or mechanical device which permits the tracking of the movement of a person or object." 18 U.S.C. §3117(b). This definition is integral to understanding whether a warrant is needed to obtain locational information from a cell phone; some courts treat cell phones as tracking devices, while others do not.

[49] Communications Assistance for Law Enforcement Act, P.L. 103-414, 108 Stat. 4279 (1994).

[50] H.Rept. 103-827, at 10 (1994).

[51] 47 U.S.C. §1002(a)(2) (2006).

[52] 47 U.S.C. §1002(a)(2)(B).

[53] This framework is described in *In re Application for Pen Register and Trap/Trace Device With Cell Site Location Authority*, 396 F. Supp. 2d 747, 753 (S.D. Tex. 2005).

[54] Orin S. Kerr, *Internet Surveillance Law After the USA Patriot Act: The Big Brother That Isn't*, 97 NW. U. L. REV. 607, 630 (2003).

[55] 18 U.S.C. §2518 (2006).

[56] 18 U.S.C. §3117 (2006). Probable cause, as required for a wiretap or information from a tracking device, is the highest level of evidentiary proof to conduct a search. It is rooted in the text of the Constitution, U.S. CONST. amend IV, and the Court has reiterated time and again that law enforcement must obtain a warrant based upon probable cause unless the investigation does not implicate a reasonable expectation of privacy or else falls within an established exception. Katz v. United States, 389 U.S. 347, 357 (1967) (citations omitted). There are various formulations of this standard, but it is said that "[p]robable cause exists where the facts and circumstances within their [the officers']knowledge and of which they had reasonably trustworthy information [are] sufficient in themselves to warrant a man of reasonable caution in the belief that an offense has been or is being committed." Brinegar v. United States, 338 U.S.160, 175-76 (1949) (citation omitted) (internal quotation marks omitted). The Court later simplified this phrase by requiring a "fair probability that contraband or evidence of a crime will be found in a particular place." Illinois v.Gates, 462 U.S. 213, 238 (1983).

[57] 18 U.S.C. §2703(d) (2006). "Specific and articulable facts" is comparable to the "reasonable suspicion" standard, which was first announced in *Terry v. Ohio*, 392 U.S. 1, 30-31 (1968). Reasonable suspicion requires that the officer "be able to articulate something more than an inchoate and unparticularized suspicion or hunch," United States v. Sokolow, 490 U.S. 1, 7 (1989) (internal quotation marks omitted), but instead has information that a "reasonably

prudent man in the circumstances would be warranted in the belief that his safety or that of others was in danger." *Terry*, 392 U.S. at 27.

[58] 18 U.S.C. §3122(b)(2) (2006). The standard for pen registers and trap and trace devices bears some resemblance to the "special needs" doctrine, which covers cases "beyond the normal need of law enforcement." Nat'l Treasury Emps. Union v. Von Raab, 489 U.S. 656, 665 (1989) (balancing the "individual's privacy expectations against the Government's interests to determine whether it is impractical to require a warrant or some level of individualized suspicion in the particular context"). This reasonableness standard has been used in cases of drug tests for high school students, Bd. of Educ. of Indep. Sch. Dist. No. 92 v. Earls, 536 U.S. 822, 838 (2002), and railroad employees, Skinner v. Ry. Labor Execs.' Ass'n., 489 U.S. 602, 633-34 (1989), and drunk driving checkpoints, Michigan Dep't of State Police v. Sitz, 496 U.S. 444, 455 (1990). But the Court has cabined off the use of this lowest standard to those few limited instances; the Court declined to apply it to a drug interdiction checkpoint, City of Indianapolis v. Edmond, 531 U.S. 32, 48 (2000), and drug tests for birthing mothers, Ferguson v. City of Charleston, 532 U.S. 67, 86-87 (2001). This balancing test is much easier to satisfy than probable cause or reasonable suspicion.

[59] *In re* Application of the United States of America for an Order for Disclosure of Telecommunications Records and Authorizing the Use of a Pen Register and Trap and Trace, 405 F. Supp. 2d 435, 439 (S.D.N.Y. 2005).

[60] *See* Congressional Distribution Memorandum, *Legal Standard for Disclosure of Cell-Site Information (CSI) and Geolocation Information*, by Gina Stevens, Alison Smith, and Jordan Segall (on file with CRS). The debate in the federal courts centers around cell site location information, which is one of the two distinct methods for determining the location of a cell phone. (A full description of cell phone technology is beyond the scope of this report, but can be found at Marshall Brain et al., *How Cell Phones Work*, HOW STUFF WORKS (last visited October 20, 2011), http://electronics.howstuffworks.com/cell-phone.htm). GPS, or Global Positioning System, is a system of 24 satellites that constantly orbit Earth. *In re* Application of the United States of America for Historical Cell Site Data, 747 F. Supp. 2d 827, 831 (S.D. Tex. 2010). When hardware inside the cell phone receives signals from at least four of these satellites, the handset can calculate its latitude and longitude to within 10 meters. *Id.* at 832. There are drawbacks to GPS technology: the system is not fully operable when objects block its access. Note, *Who Knows Where You've Been? Privacy Concerns Regarding the Use of Cellular Phones as Personal Locators*, 18 HARV. J. L. & TECH. 307, 308 (2004). Despite the accuracy of this technology, courts have yet to address whether GPS tracking can be used to locate a cell phone's location. Adam B. Merrill, Comment, *Can You Find Me Now? The Federal Government's Attempt to Track Criminal Suspects Using Their Cell Phones*, 43 ARIZ. ST. L. J. 591, 606 (2011).

The second method of determining the location of a cell phone is by triangulation, a process by which a cell phone's location can be determined from its communication with local cell towers. *See In re* Pen Register & Trap/Trace Device with Cell Site Location Authority, 396 F. Supp. 2d 747, 751 (S.D. Tex. 2005). There are two distinct technologies used to locate a cell phone through a network: time difference of arrival and the angle of arrival. Note, *Who Knows Where You've Been?*, 18 HARV. J. L. & TECH. 307, 308 (2004). The time difference technology measures the time it takes for a signal to travel from the cell phone to the tower. When multiple towers pick up this signal, an algorithm allows the network to determine the phone's latitude and longitude. *Id.* at 308-09. The angle of arrival technology uses the angles at which a phone's signal reaches a station. When more than one tower receives the signal, the network compares this data the multiple angles of arrival and triangulates the location of the cell phone. *Id.* at 309.

[61] *In Re* Application of the United States for an Order for Prospective Cell Site Location Information on a Certain Cellular Telephone, 460 F. Supp. 2d 448, 452 (S.D.N.Y. 2006) (quoting Gov. Br. at 2).

[62] *Cell Tracking*, ELECTRONIC FRONTIER FOUNDATION, https://www.eff.org/issues/cell-tracking (last visited October 19, 2011); *see also* Brian C. Davis, Note, *An Un-Watchful Eye: How Courts Have Allowed Emerging Electronic Surveillance Escape Fourth Amendment Protection*, 46 NEW ENG. L. REV. (Forthcoming 2012) (on file with the New England Law Review) ("[I]f the government decides to use these devices, they must comply with the safeguards entrenched in the Fourth Amendment.").

[63] Some cases hold that historical but not prospective information can be obtained under the Stored Communications Act. *See In re* Application for Pen Register and Trap/Trace Device with Cell Location Authority, 396 F. Supp. 2d 747 (S.D. Tex. 2005); *In re* United States for an Order (1) Authorizing the Use of a Pen Register and a Trap and Trace Device and (2) Authorizing Release of Subscriber Information and/or Cell Site Information, 396 F. Supp. 2d 294 (E.D.N.Y. 2005). Others hold that historical information and limited prospective information can be obtained under the SCA. *See In re* Application of the United States of America for an Order: (1) Authorizing the Installation and Use of a Pen Register and Trap and Trace Device, and (2) Authorizing Release of Subscriber and Other Information, 622 F. Supp. 2d 411 (S.D. Tex. 2007). Finally, others permit access to both prospective and historical information. *See In re* Application of the United States for an Order for Prospective Cell Site Location Information on a Certain Cellular Telephone, 460 F. Supp. 2d 448 (S.D.N.Y. 2006).

[64] The information sought in this case was not from a GPS device; the court was not asked nor did it take a position on the use of GPS data, but merely answered the cell location information question. *In re* Application of the United States of America for an Order Directing a Provider of Electronic Communication Service to Disclose Records to the Government, 620 F.3d 304, 311 (3d Cir. 2010).

[65] *Id.* at 305.

[66] *In re* Application of the United States of America for an Order Directing Provider of Electronic Communication Service to Disclosure Records to the Government, 534 F. Supp. 2d 585, 585-86 (W.D. Pa. 2008).

[67] *In re* Application of the United States of America for an Order Directing Provider of Electronic Communication Service to Disclose Records to the Government, No. 07-524M, 2008 U.S. Dist. LEXIS 98761 (W.D. Pa. September 10, 2008).

[68] *Application for Disclosure of Records*, 620 F.3d at 319.

[69] *Application for Disclosure of Records*, 534 F. Supp. 2d at 601.

[70] 18 U.S.C. §3117(b).

[71] To be clear, the definition of "electronic communications" excludes "any communication from a tracking device," 18 U.S.C. §2510(12)(C). The definition of "wire communications," the other form of communications governed by the Stored Communications Act, does not exclude communications from a tracking device. 18 U.S.C. §2510(1).

[72] *Application for Disclosure of Records*, 534 F. Supp. 2d at 601 (quoting 18 U.S.C. §3117(b)).

[73] *Id.* at 602.

[74] *Id.*

[75] *Id.* at 601.

[76] *Application for Disclosure of Records*, 620 F.3d at 319.

[77] ECPA defines "electronic communication" as "any transfer of signs, signals, writing, images, sounds, data, or intelligence of any nature transmitted in whole or in part by a wire, radio, electromagnetic, photoelectronic or photooptical system that affects interstate or foreign commerce." 18 U.S.C. §2510(12).

[78] *Id.* at 309.

[79] 18 U.S.C. §2510(1). "'Aural transfer' means a transfer containing the human voice at any point...." §2510(18). Meanwhile, "electronic communication" does not include "any wire or oral communication...." §2510(12). "Oral communication" means an utterance by a person with a justifiable expectation that the communication will not be intercepted. §2510(2).

[80] *Application for Disclosure of Records*, 620 F.3d at 310.

[81] *Id.*

[82] *Id.* at 315. This interpretation of §2703(d) has not gone unscathed. Professor Orin Kerr regards this theory as "quite unpersuasive." Orin Kerr, *Third Circuit Rules that Magistrate Judges Have Discretion to Reject non-Warrant Court Order Applications and Require Search Warrants to Obtain Historical Cell-Site Records*, THE VOLOKH CONSPIRACY, http://volokh.com/2010/09/08/third-circuit-rules-that-magistrate-judges-have-discretion-to-reject-court-order-application-and-require-search-warrants-to-obtain-historical-cell-site-records/ (last visited October 4, 2011). Kerr cites to *Ex parte United States*, 287 U.S. 241 (1932), noting that "magistrate judges do not have discretion to decide whether to issue court orders if the government satisfies the legal threshold." *Id.* If the court were given discretion whether to require a warrant, law enforcement could then forum shop for the more lenient magistrate. *Id.*

[83] *In re* Application for Pen Register and Trap/Trace Device with Cell Site Location Authority, 396 F. Supp. 2d 747, 759, n.16 (S.D. Tex. 2005) (noting that historical cell location, as compared to prospective information, fits the definition of transactional records covered by the Stored Communications Act).

[84] *Id.* (citing 18 U.S.C. §3117(b) (2006)).

[85] *Id.* at 755.

[86] *Id.* at 757-58 ("With regard to information acquired solely pursuant to the authority for pen registers and trap and trace devices ... such call identifying information shall not include any information that may disclose the physical location of the subscriber (except to the extent that the location may be determined from the telephone number).") (emphasis in original) (quoting 47 U.S.C. §1002(a)(2)).

[87] *In re Application*, 396 F. Supp. 2d at 758.

[88] 18 U.S.C. §2510(15).

[89] *Id.* at 759.

[90] *Id.* at 759, 765.

[91] *See In re* Application of the United States for an Order for Prospective Cell Site Location Information on a Certain Cellular Telephone, 2006 U.S. Dist. LEXIS 11747, *2 (S.D.N.Y. 2006); *In re* Application of the United States of America for an Order Authorizing the Disclosure of Prospective Cell Site Information, 412 F. Supp 2d 947 (E.D. Wis.2006); *In re* Application for Pen Register and Trap/Trace Device With Cell Site Location Authority, 396 F. Supp. 2d294 (E.D.N.Y. 2005); *In re* Application of the United States of America for an Order (1) Authorizing the Use of a Pen Register and a Trap and Trace Device and (2) Authorizing Release of Subscriber Information and/or Cell Site Information, 384 F. Supp. 2d 562 (E.D.N.Y. 2005).

[92] See Lisa M. Lindemenn, Note, *From Cell to Slammer: Flaws in the Hybrid Theory*, 53 ARIZ. L. REV. 663, 672 (2011).

[93] 18 U.S.C. §3127(3)-(4) (2006).

[94] *In re* Application of the United States of America for an Order for Disclosure of Telecommunications Records and Authorizing the Use of a Pen Register and Trap and Trace, 405 F. Supp. 2d 435, 438 (S.D.N.Y. 2005); 18 U.S.C.§3127(3)-(4)

[95] Uniting and Strengthening America by Providing Appropriate Tools Required to Intercept and Obstruct Terrorism(USA PATRIOT ACT) Act of 2001, P.L. 107-56, §216(c)(2), 115 Stat. 272, 290.

[96] 18 U.S.C. §3123(a)(1) (2006).

[97] 47 U.S.C. §1002. This section reads, in pertinent part:

a telecommunications carrier shall ensure that its equipment, facilities, or services that provide a customer or subscriber with the ability to originate, terminate, or direct communications are capable of—...

(2) expeditiously isolating and enabling the government, pursuant to a court order or other lawful authorization, to access call-indentifying information that is reasonably available to the carrier—

(A) before, during, or immediately after the transmission of a wire or electronic communication (or such later time as may be acceptable to the government); and

(B) in a manner that allows it to be associated to which it pertains,

except that, with regard to information acquired *solely pursuant* to the authority for pen registers and trap and trace devices (as defined in section 3127 of Title 18), and such call identifying information *shall not include any information that may disclose the physical location of the subscriber* (except to the extent that the location may be determined from the telephone number); (emphasis added).

[98] 18 U.S.C. §2703(c)(1) (2006).

[99] *In re Application for Disclosure of Telecommunications Records*, 405 F. Supp. 2d at 444-45.

[100] 18 U.S.C. §2510(12) (2006).

[101] *In re Application for Disclosure of Telecommunications Records*, 405 F. Supp. 2d at 446.

[102] *In re* Application for Pen Register and Trap/Trace Device With Cell Site Location Authority, 396 F. Supp. 2d 747, 753 (S.D. Tex. 2005).

[103] *See* Lindemenn, *supra* note 92, at 675.

[104] *See In re* Application of the United States for an Order: (1) Authorizing the Installation and Use of a Pen Register and Trap and Trace Device; and (2) Authorizing Release of Subscriber Information and/or Cell-Site Information, 411 F. Supp. 2d 678, 680 (W.D. La. 2006); *In re* Application of the United States for an Order for Prospective Cell Site Location Information on a Certain Cellular Telephone, 460 F. Supp. 2d 448 (S.D.N.Y. 2006).

[105] *In re* Applications of the United States for Orders Authorizing the Disclosure of Cell Site Information, Nos. 05-403, 05-404, 05-407, 05-408, 05-409, 05-410, 05-411, 2005 WL 3658531, at *1 (D.D.C. October 26, 2005); *In re* Application of the United States of America for an Order Authorizing the Installation and Use of a Pen Register a Caller Identification System on Telephone Numbers [Sealed] and [Sealed] and the Production of Real Time Cell Site Information, 402 F. Supp. 2d 597 (D. MD. 2005); *In re* Application of the United States for and Order for Prospective Cell Site Location Information on a Certain Cellular Telephone, No. 06 CRIM. MISC. 01, 2006 WL 468300, at *2 (S.D.N.Y. February 28, 2006); *In re* Application of the United States of America for an Order Authorizing the Disclosure of Prospective Cell Site Information, 412 F. Supp. 2d 947, 949 (E.D. Wis. 2006).

[106] The Director of the Federal Bureau of Investigation (FBI) testified before Congress during its consideration of CALEA, and insisted that the Pen Register/Trap Trace Statute has "'nothing to do with' the Stored Communications Act, and that transactional information is 'exclusively dealt with in chapter 121 of Title 18.'" *In re Application*, 396 F. Supp. 2d 747, 753 (S.D. Tex. 2005) ("The government's hybrid theory, while undeniably creative, amounts to little more than a retrospective assemblage of disparate statutory parts to achieve a desired result."); *see Digital Telephony and Law Enforcement Access to Advanced Telecommunications Technologies and Services: Joint Hearings Before the Subcomm. on Technology and Law of the Senate Committee on the Judiciary and the Subcomm. on Civil and Constitutional Rights of the House Committee on the Judiciary*, 103rd Cong. 32 (statement of Director Freeh):

First, as is clearly set forth in the "purpose" section of the proposed legislation, the intent of the legislation is to maintain existing technical capabilities and to "clarify and define the responsibilities of common carriers *** to provide the assistance required to ensure that government agencies can implement court orders and lawful authorizations to intercept the content of wire and electronic communications and acquire call setup information *under chapters 119 and 206 of Title 18 and chapter 36 of Title 50.*" (emphasis added.) These chapters have nothing to do with "transactional information" under our federal electronic surveillance and privacy laws. All telecommunications "transactional" information is already protected by federal law and is exclusively dealt with in chapter 121 of Title 18 of the United States Code ("stored wire and electronic communications and transactional records access"). The proposed legislation does not relate to chapter 121 of Title 18. Second, under federal law, Congress treats law enforcement's use of pen registers and dialing information differently than "transactional information"—such as detailed telephone *billing* information.

[107] Susan Freiwald, *Cell Phone Location Data and the Fourth Amendment: A Question of Law*, Not Fact, 70 MD. L. REV. 681, 681 (2011).

[108] CRS Report R41663, *Law Enforcement Use of Global Positioning (GPS) Devices to Monitor Motor Vehicles: Fourth Amendment Considerations*, by Alison M. Smith.

[109] United States v. Knotts, 460 U.S. 276, 278-79 (1983).

[110] *Id.* at 279.

[111] *Id.*

[112] *Id.* at 281.

[113] *Id.* at 285.

[114] United States v. Karo, 468 U.S. 705, 714 (1984). Though the monitoring of the can of ether while in the private residence was deemed unconstitutional, the warrant permitting police to search the residence where the contraband was found was upheld because the police had sufficient untainted evidence independent of this monitoring. *Id.* at 721.

[115] *Id.* at 708.

[116] *Id.* at 710.

[117] *Id.* at 714.

[118] *Id.* at 716.

[119] *Id.* at 715.

[120] United States v. Garcia, 474 F.3d 994, 997 (7th Cir. 2007).

[121] *Id.*

[122] United States v. Pineda-Moreno, 591 F.3d 1212, 1213 (9th Cir. 2010).

[123] *Id.* at 1216.

[124] *Id.*

[125] United States v. Maynard, 615 F.3d 544 (D.C. Cir. 2010), *cert. granted sub nom.* United States v. Jones, 131 S. Ct. 3064 (2011) (No. 10-1259).

[126] Brief for Respondent at 4, *Jones*, 131 S. Ct. 3064 (2011) (No. 10-1259), 2011 WL 4479076.

[127] Brief for Petitioner at 3-4, *Jones*, 131 S. Ct. 3064 (2011) (No. 10-1259), 2011 WL 3561881.

[128] Brief for Respondent, *supra* note 126, at 5.

[129] United States v. Jones, 451 F. Supp. 2d 71, 88 (D.D.C. 2006).

[130] United States v. Maynard, 615 F.3d 544, 555-56 (D.C. Cir. 2010).

[131] *Id.* at 556.

[132] Brief for Appellants at 65 n.239, *Maynard*, 615 F.3d 544 (D.C. Cir. 2010) (Nos. 08-3030, 08-3034), 2009 WL 3155141 (quoting Recent Case, *Constitutional Law—Fourth Amendment—Seventh Circuit Holds that GPS Tracking is Not a Search.—United States v. Garcia, 474 F.3d 994 (7th Cir. 2007), Reh'g and Suggestion for Reh'g Denied, No. 06-2741, 2007 U.S. App. LEXIS 8397 (7th Cir. Mar. 29, 2007)*, 120 Harv. L. Rev. 2230, 2235 (2007))

[133] United States v. Knotts, 460 U.S. 276, 284 (1983).

[134] *Maynard*, 615 F.3d at 563.

[135] United States v. Maynard, 615 F.3d 544, 555-56 (D.C. Cir. 2010), *cert. granted sub nom. United States v. Jones*, 131 S. Ct. 3064 (2011) (No. 10-1259) (oral argument held on November 8, 2011).

[136] It should be noted that this passage was dicta, meaning it is not controlling but merely persuasive.

[137] Brief for Petitioner, *supra* note 127, at 34.

[138] Brief for Respondent, supra note 126, at 44 fn.8 (citing The Living Webster Encyclopedic Dictionary of the English Language 300 (1975)).

[139] Brief for Petitioner, *supra* note 127, at 19.
[140] United States v. McIver, 186 F.3d 1119, 1126-27 (9th Cir. 1999).
[141] United States v. Michael, 645 F.2d 252, 256 (5th Cir. 1981).
[142] United States v. Moore, 562 F.2d 106, 112-113 (1st Cir. 1977).
[143] Senator Al Franken has introduced the Location Privacy and Protection Act of 2011 (S. 1223)—similar to the GPS bill, but which applies only to private, not governmental, actors. Because it only applies to private actors, and this report focuses on governmental tracking, it will not be discussed.
[144] DIGITAL DUE PROCESS, http://www.digitaldueprocess.com (last visited October 19, 2011). The group's official mission statement is "to simplify, clarify, and unify the ECPA standards, providing stronger privacy protections for communications and associated data in response to changes in technology and new services and usage patterns, while preserving the legal tools necessary for government agencies to enforce the laws, respond to emergency circumstances and protect the public." *Id.* at http://www.digitaldueprocess.org/ index.cfm?objectid=99629E40-2551-11DF-8E02000C296BA163.
[145] The Electronic Communications Privacy Act: Government Perspectives on Protecting Privacy in the Digital Age, 112th Cong. (2011) (statement of James A. Baker, Assoc. Dep. Att'y Gen., Dep't of Justice) ("Courts' conflicting interpretations of the statutory basis for obtaining prospective cell-site information have created uncertainty regarding the proper standard for compelled disclosure of cell-location information, and some courts' requirement of probable cause has hampered the government's ability to obtain important information in investigations of serious crimes. Legislation to clarify and unify the legal standard and the proper mechanism for obtaining prospective cell-site information could eliminate this uncertainty.").
[146] Though this bill targets both governmental and private, third-party use of geolocation information, the private use is beyond the scope of this report.
[147] S. 1011, 112th Cong., 1st Sess. (2011).
[148] 18 U.S.C. §2703(c).
[149] S. 1212, H.R. 2168, 112th Cong., 1st Sess. (2011).
[150] S. 1212, §5.
[151] "Geolocation information" is defined as "any information, that is not the content of a communication, concerning the location of a wireless communication device or tracking device (as that term is defined section 3117) that, in whole or in part, is generated by or derived from the operation of that device and that could be used to determine or infer information regarding the location of the person." S. 1212, §2601(4). "Geolocation information" covers information from both GPS tracking and tracking via cell site location information.
[152] The bill prohibits use of this information by "any person" (e.g., individuals, telecommunications companies, Internet service providers, website operators, etc.), and not solely government actors. However, private use of geolocation information is beyond the scope of this report; this analysis of S. 1212 is limited to government access to geolocation information.
[153] S. 1212, §2602(a)(1). Currently there is no broad federal prohibition against the use of geolocation information.
[154] "Geolocation information service" is defined as "the provision of a global positioning service or other mapping, locational, or directional information service to the public, or to such class of users as to be effectively available to the public, by or through the operation of any wireless communication device, including any mobile telephone, global positioning system receiving device, mobile computer, or other similar or successor device." S. 1212, §2601(5).
[155] Unlike landline phones in a person's house, the police can only determine a cell phone caller's location either by the caller telling the police where he is located, or by using the geolocation information from the phone.

[156] Kyllo v. United States, 533 U.S. 27, 34 (2001).
[157] Kevin McLaughlin, *The Fourth Amendment and Cell Phone Location Tracking: Where are We?*, 29 HASTINGS COMM. & ENT. L. J. 421, 428 (2007).

In: Legalities of GPS and Cell Phone Surveillance ISBN: 978-1-62257-026-3
Editors: E. Johnson and M. Rodriguez

Chapter 3

UNITED STATES V. JONES: GPS MONITORING, PROPERTY, AND PRIVACY*

Richard M. Thompson II

SUMMARY

In *United States v. Jones*, 132 S. Ct. 945 (2012), all nine Supreme Court Justices agreed that Jones was *searched* when the police attached a Global Positioning System (GPS) device to the undercarriage of his car and tracked his movements for four weeks. The Court, however, splintered on what constituted the search: the attachment of the device or the long-term monitoring. The majority held that the *attachment* of the GPS device and an attempt to obtain information was the violation; Justice Alito, concurring, argued that the *monitoring* was a violation of Jones's reasonable expectation of privacy; and Justice Sotomayor, also concurring, agreed with them both, but would provide further Fourth Amendment protections. This report will examine these three decisions in an effort to find their place in the body of existing Fourth Amendment law pertaining to privacy, property, and technology.

In *Jones*, the police attached a GPS tracking device to the bottom of Jones's car and monitored his movements for 28 days. At trial, the prosecution relied on Jones's movements to a stash house to tie him to a

---

* This is an edited, reformatted and augmented version of Congressional Research Service, Publication No. R42511, dated April 30, 2012.

drug conspiracy. Jones was convicted and given a life sentence. The United States Court of Appeals for the District of Columbia Circuit reversed, holding that the evidence was unlawfully obtained under the Fourth Amendment. The Supreme Court agreed. The majority, speaking through Justice Scalia, explained that a physical intrusion into a constitutionally protected area, coupled with an attempt to obtain information, can constitute a violation of the Fourth Amendment. Although the Court's landmark decision in *Katz v. United States*, 389 U.S. 347 (1967), supposedly altered the focus of the Fourth Amendment from property to privacy, the majority argued that it left untouched traditional spheres of Fourth Amendment protection—a person and his house, papers, and effects. Because the police had invaded Jones's property—his car, which is an *effect*—that was all the Court needed to hold that a constitutional search had occurred.

The majority's test, however, provides little guidance in instances where the government need not physically install a device to conduct surveillance, for instance, by using cell phones or preinstalled GPS devices in vehicles.

To understand how the Court may rule on these technologies, one must look to the two concurrences, which provide a more global interpretation of the Fourth Amendment. Justice Alito, writing for a four-member concurrence, would have applied the *Katz* privacy formulation, asserting that longer-term monitoring constitutes an invasion of privacy, whereas short-term monitoring does not. He left it to future courts to distinguish between the two.

Justice Sotomayor's concurrence appears to provide the most protection, finding that both the trespass approach and the privacy-based approach should be utilized. She also questioned the rule that any information provided to a third party, which occurs in many commercial transactions like banking or computing, should lose all privacy protections.

Although all three opinions concluded that the government's action in *Jones* was a search, none expressly required that police get a warrant in future GPS tracking cases. (The government forfeited the argument.) Further, there is no clear indication of the level of suspicion—probable cause, reasonable suspicion, or something less—that is required to attach a GPS unit and monitor the target's movements. Additionally, there have been several bills filed in the 112th Congress, including Senator Patrick J. Leahy's Electronic Communications Privacy Act Amendment Act of 2011 (S. 1011) and Senator Ron Wyden's and Representative Jason Chaffetz's identical legislation, S. 1212 and H.R. 2168, the Geolocational Privacy and Surveillance Act (GPS bill), that would require a warrant based upon probable cause to access geolocation information.

INTRODUCTION

There is little doubt that technology is fast becoming intertwined with our jobs, our social life, and even our most private interactions with each other. This phenomenon creates friction among many compelling interests. The first is a clash between two contrasting values: the desire for privacy and the longing to be connected through the newest and most advanced technology. To a certain extent, as one advances, the other must necessarily recede. Meanwhile, courts are tasked with determining the balance between government's law enforcement needs and the people's privacy. The Fourth Amendment to the U.S. Constitution provides the measuring stick to determine this balance. The amendment ensures "[t]he right of the people to be secure in their persons, houses, papers, and effects, against unreasonable searches and seizures, shall not be violated."[1] Its primary function is to prohibit government intrusion upon the privacy and property rights of the people. When new technology is involved, achieving this balance is not an easy undertaking.

United States v. Jones presented such a challenge to the Supreme Court. The question posed was whether the installation and month-long monitoring of a GPS device attached to Jones's car constituted a violation of the Fourth Amendment's prohibition against "unreasonable searches and seizures."[2] This usage of the Global Positioning System (GPS)[3] is not unusual in criminal investigations,[4] but up to that point longer-term monitoring had not been directly tested by the Court. Thus, many observers awaited the *Jones* ruling for its potential impact not only on government monitoring programs, but also on general Fourth Amendment cases involving prolonged government surveillance.

In prior government tracking cases,[5] the Court applied the test from *Katz v. United States*, which addresses whether the individual had a reasonable expectation of privacy in the area to be searched.[6] Because the police in *Jones* physically invaded his property to attach the GPS device—whereas in the previous cases they had not—the Court declined to apply *Katz*, but instead based its decision on a trespass theory.[7] The trespass theory asks whether there was a physical intrusion onto a constitutionally protected area coupled with an attempt to obtain information.[8] In *Jones*, there was, so the Court applied this more limited test and held that a search occurred. Though the majority bypassed the *Katz* approach, Justice Alito, concurring with Justices Breyer, Ginsburg, and Kagan, would have applied *Katz*.[9] Long-term surveillance, Justice Alito wrote, violated Jones's reasonable expectation of privacy under *Katz*. Justice Sotomayor agreed with both the majority and Alito's concurrence, but called for additional protection by questioning the viability of the third-party doctrine, which holds that any information voluntarily given to a third party loses all privacy protections.[10]

This report will analyze all three opinions in an attempt to determine how *Jones* might affect future use of GPS tracking and other government surveillance techniques. First, it will briefly recount the facts that led to Jones's prosecution, his appeal, and the Supreme Court's review. Next, it will analyze the majority's property-based test, evaluating it against similar Fourth Amendment case law. Additionally, this section will raise issues concerning the possible impact of this approach on similar search and seizure cases. Next, the report will examine both Justice Alito's and Justice Sotomayor's concurrences and their potential impact on cases involving technology. Because the Court did not express whether a warrant is required, the report will posit several theories on how this issue may be resolved in the future.

UNITED STATES V. JONES: A PROPERTY-BASED APPROACH TO THE FOURTH AMENDMENT

In 2004, a Joint Task Force of the FBI and the District of Columbia Metropolitan Police Department suspected Antoine Jones was part of a drug distribution ring.[11] Based on information obtained from wiretaps, a pen register,[12] and video surveillance, the task force obtained a warrant to monitor Jones's Jeep with a GPS tracking device. According to the terms of the warrant, the officers had 10 days to install it and were required to do it in the District of Columbia. The officers installed the device on the 11th day in Maryland while the Jeep was parked in a public parking lot.[13] For the next four weeks the device tracked Jones's every movement, creating 2,000 pages of monitoring data.[14] During this time, the device tracked Jones's movements to and from a known stash house.

Jones was indicted for conspiracy to distribute and possession with intent to distribute cocaine. At trial, the prosecution relied heavily on Jones's movements derived from the GPS to connect him with a larger drug ring.[15] He moved to dismiss this information as a warrantless search under the Fourth Amendment. The United States District Court for the District of Columbia excluded the data derived when his car was parked in his garage but allowed into evidence all of his public movements.[16] Jones was ultimately convicted and sentenced to life imprisonment.[17] The United States Court of Appeals for the District of Columbia Circuit reversed, holding that the GPS data were derived in violation of Jones's reasonable expectation of privacy under the Fourth Amendment.[18] The Supreme Court then granted a writ of certiorari, agreeing to review Jones's case.

Most observers assumed the Supreme Court would, like the D.C. Circuit Court of Appeals, apply the reasonable expectation of privacy test developed in *Katz v. United States* to determine if the tracking was a Fourth Amendment search. Under the *Katz* test, a search in the constitutional sense has occurred if the individual had an actual expectation of privacy in the area to be searched that society would deem reasonable.[19] Since 1967, when *Katz* was handed down, the Court had developed a body of case law applying this privacy-based formulation of the Fourth Amendment.[20]

The *Jones* majority, led by Justice Scalia, took a different route.[21] It held that the *attachment* of the GPS device, coupled with its use to monitor Jones's movements, was a constitutional search.[22] The Fourth Amendment ensures that "[t]he right of the people to be secure in their persons, houses, papers, and effects, against unreasonable searches and seizures, shall not be violated."[23] Because Jones's vehicle is an *effect*—listed in the text of the Fourth Amendment—the police's physical intrusion by attaching the GPS for tracking purposes constituted a *search*.[24] This theory hinges on common law trespass as it was known in 1791 (when the Fourth Amendment was adopted). It does not rely on *Katz*, nor any subjective conception of privacy. The majority contended that Jones's rights should not strictly depend on whether his reasonably expected zone of privacy was pierced.[25] Rather, the majority asserted, property rights also define an individual's right to be free from government intrusion.

Justice Alito, in concurrence, contended that the majority's reliance on "18th-century tort law" which "might have provided grounds in 1791 for a suit based on trespass to chattels," "strains the language of the Fourth Amendment; it has little if any support in current Fourth Amendment case law; and it is highly artificial."[26] Justice Alito would have instead applied the *Katz* formulation.[27]

This criticism prompts two central questions: (1) Does the majority's property-based approach enjoy textual, historical, or jurisprudential support?; and (2) What effect will this approach have on other areas of government investigations?

The seeds for the property-based approach were planted in England in *Entick v. Carrington*, a case considered by many as an ancestor of the Fourth Amendment.[28] There, the English court forbade government agents from searching through Entick's home, looking for papers intended to prove his seditious writing. The agents had a general warrant to search the home, but the warrant lacked a specific description of the area to be searched and the items to be seized. Lord Camden declared that no government agent nor any other person may enter the property of another without permission, even if no harm is done.[29] This theory carried over to the colonies and prompted the framers to include a prohibition against unreasonable searches and seizures when drafting the Bill of Rights.[30] Under this common law trespass approach, the key inquiry is not necessarily the content of the information obtained by the police, but rather their method of retrieving it. The *Jones* Court had no doubts that the attachment of the GPS device (which required a trespass of Jones's car) would have been a search when the Fourth Amendment was adopted—when *Entick* was fresh in the framers' minds.[31]

Although property certainly controlled Fourth Amendment thinking during the infancy of the Fourth Amendment, its control waned in later years. *Olmstead v. United States* provides an example. There, federal agents installed several wiretaps on the telephone wires coming from Olmstead's house.[32] In upholding this electronic eavesdropping, the Court ruled that the Fourth Amendment applied only when there was an official search or seizure of a person, his tangible papers and effects, and an "actual physical invasion" of the individual's home.[33] Because the installation of the wiretap did not require the agents to trespass onto Olmstead's property, the Court held that it was not a search or seizure under the Fourth Amendment.[34]

Forty years later, the Court began its shift away from this property-centric approach. In *Warden v. Hayden*, the Court noted the property-based approach had been discredited over the years, and that privacy should be the focus of the inquiry under the Fourth Amendment.[35] Subsequently, the Court decided *Katz v. United States*, where it held an electronic surveillance of Katz's conversations while he was in a public telephone booth was impermissible, despite the fact that no property rights were involved.[36] The "Fourth Amendment protects people, not places," the Court declared, and any search that invaded a person's "reasonable expectation of privacy" should be considered a search in the constitutional sense.[37]

This seemingly conflicting line of cases left many wondering whether property and privacy could coexist under the Fourth Amendment. The Court attempted to reconcile these two lines in *Soldal v. County of Cook*.[38] There, while under the supervision of local police, a landlord had his tenant's trailer home towed from the rented lot.[39] The tenant sued the police under Section 1983, a civil rights statute, for a violation of his Fourth Amendment right to be free from unreasonable seizure. The Seventh Circuit Court of Appeals denied the tenant's claim, holding that any Fourth Amendment violation must be supported by some invasion of privacy.[40] The police did not invade the tenant's privacy, but only his possessory interest in the property, enough for the court to hold the Fourth Amendment inapplicable. Instead, the panel noted that the due process clause was the proper avenue of relief for a "pure deprivation of property."[41]

The Supreme Court disagreed, ruling that the police action was a seizure notwithstanding the lack of a privacy interest at stake.[42] The Court took pains to note that privacy-based cases like *Katz* and *Warden* had not "snuffed out the previously recognized protection for property under the Fourth Amendment," but instead had "demonstrated that property is not the sole measure of Fourth Amendment violations."[43] The Court noted that the amendment does not protect possessory interests in all kinds of property, such as an open field not closely connected with a person's home, but certainly covers things specifically listed in the constitutional text—persons, houses, papers, and effects.[44]

This idea that the Fourth Amendment protects both privacy and property independently is infused throughout the majority opinion in *Jones*. As Justice Scalia noted, *Katz* did not *supplant* the common law trespass approach, but merely *supplemented* it.[45] But is a simple trespass alone enough to constitute a violation? The Court answered no: in addition to the physical intrusion, there must be "an attempt to find something or to obtain information."[46] Also, not every police trespass will be a constitutional search. The government must intrude upon an area enumerated in the text of the amendment (person, houses, papers, and effects).[47] This leaves several questions. If a car is an effect, what other personal property may be covered under this approach? Will computer data constitute an *effect*? Will an e-mail constitute an electronic *paper*? If a police officer walks onto one's porch, is that an invasion of his *house*? There are no easy answers to these questions.

Additionally, because the Court focused on the attachment of the device and the property interests involved, there remain questions of whether prolonged tracking with a device is permissible under the Fourth Amendment if there is no trespass.

As the majority noted, "[s]ituations involving merely transmission of electronic signals without trespass would *remain* subject to *Katz* analysis."[48] Justice Alito's and Sotomayor's concurrences in *Jones* may be scrutinized for how the Court might handle these scenarios under *Katz*.[49]

The Implications of Jones and Technology

As more cell phones and cars are outfitted with GPS tracking technologies, police need not physically attach a device to track its movements. Because the *Jones* majority opinion is based on a *physical* trespass into a constitutionally protected area, it seemingly will not apply where GPS is preinstalled. Justices Alito, and his four-Justice concurrence, and Sotomayor, concurring separately, provide insight into how a future court may apply the Fourth Amendment to evolving technologies.[50] These opinions rely, to a certain extent, on the mosaic theory first discussed in the D.C. Circuit opinion, which says that tracking a person's public movements over a long duration is constitutionally unacceptable even if tracking each of the movements individually may be permitted. Whether this approach will garner a majority on the Court is unclear. However, at a minimum, these concurrences have engendered discussion in the lower courts, with several courts citing the mosaic theory as a viable alternative.[51]

The question then becomes how much weight should the Alito and Sotomayor concurring opinions be accorded?[52] There is no *one* rule to answer this question.[53] Generally, there are two types of concurrences in Supreme Court opinions. The first is the true concurrence, in which the Justice concurs in the judgment, but disagrees with the reasoning.[54] Justice Alito's opinion exemplifies that type of concurrence; he agreed that the surveillance constituted a Fourth Amendment search, but would have decided the case under the traditional reasonable expectation of privacy test instead of the trespass test. The second category is the simple concurrence, where the Justice agrees with the judgment and the reasoning of the majority,[55] but also poses possible new theories that may not be directly relevant to that particular case, but can be used later to move the law in a particular direction.[56] Justice Sotomayor's opinion seems to fit this latter category. Although these two concurrences chart somewhat different courses in their strategy and reasoning, when combined they appear to command five votes on the Court—a potential majority.[57]

Justice Alito's Concurrence: A *Katz*-Based Approach

Justice Alito spends most of his concurrence attempting to counter the majority's common law trespass theory.[58] He argued that Scalia's reversion to the law as it stood in 1791 was unwise, and a return to the much-criticized property approach.[59] The focus of this report, however, is Justice Alito's discussion of long-term GPS tracking under *Katz*'s reasonable expectation of privacy test.

Before coming up on appeal, the D.C. Circuit below examined whether Jones's whereabouts over the month-long period of tracking were *exposed* to the public.[60] A person's movements are not *actually* exposed, the court answered, because the likelihood that anyone could actually follow someone for a month is highly improbable.[61] Further, the movements are not *constructively* exposed because in many instances the whole is greater than the sum of the parts.[62] This last proposition is premised on the mosaic theory. The mosaic theory supposes that tracking the whole of one's movements over an extended period of time reveals significantly more about that person than each individual trip does in isolation.[63] For instance, police cannot infer much about a person from *one* trip to the liquor store. However, a *daily* trip to the same liquor store would provide greater insight into the person's habits. The government has employed this theory in the national security context for protecting intelligence sources and methods of obtaining information.[64] The thrust of the argument is that unless a person has a broad view of the situation in question, he will not understand the importance of a single piece of evidence.[65] Thus, with GPS tracking, following someone for one trip may not say much about a person, but following his every movement for an extended period presumably reveals considerably more.

United States v. Knotts created an obstacle to the panel's adoption of the mosaic theory.[66] In *Knotts*, the Supreme Court held that a person has no reasonable expectation of privacy in his movements on public streets.[67] The Court, however, did not foreclose the argument that, even if traveling on public roadways, pervasive or intrusive police activity may violate the Fourth Amendment.[68] The Court suggested it would revisit the issue if police were to use "dragnet-type law enforcement practices."[69] Although the purport of this phrase is somewhat obscure, the D.C. Circuit understood it to mean that 24-hour surveillance of a single individual was sufficient for it to apply.[70] As such, the panel ruled that the previous tracking cases were not controlling, allowing it to apply the mosaic theory.[71] Based on this application, the court granted Jones's motion to dismiss all location evidence obtained from the GPS device.

As noted earlier, Justice Scalia and the majority did not apply the mosaic theory. Instead they grounded their decision in a common law trespass theory.[72] Justice Alito, on the other hand, wanted to confront directly this question of how technology affected a society's expectations of privacy. He first posited that the ubiquity of cell phones, video monitoring, and other technologies in modern life shapes the average person's expectation of privacy—presumably reducing that expectation.[73] Based on his understanding of *Katz,* Alito would have asked whether the use of GPS tracking involved an intrusion a reasonable person would not have expected. Under his approach, "relatively short-term monitoring of a person's movements on public streets accords with expectations of privacy that our society has recognized as reasonable."[74] However, the use of "longer term" GPS monitoring will in most instances violate the Fourth Amendment.[75] Justice Alito declined to create a rule for determining at what point police tracking crosses this constitutional line. He concluded that four weeks of tracking was a search.[76]

Because of the limited nature of Justice Alito's discussion, it is difficult to discern precisely which theory he employed. It is arguable that he and the three other Justices implicitly support the mosaic theory. To say that short-term monitoring is permissible, but longer-term monitoring is not, indicates there is something about the aggregation of a person's movements that prompted these Justices to deem it a Fourth Amendment search.[77] It could also be argued that Justice Alito's concurrence did not accept the mosaic theory, but instead applied the probabilistic model of Fourth Amendment theory.[78] This theory supposes that when government conducts an investigation in a way that would surprise an individual, or "interferes with customs and social expectations," it violates a reasonable expectation of privacy.[79] Justice Alito categorizes the *Katz* test as looking at the "privacy expectations of the hypothetical reasonable person"—a hypothetical person who has "a well-developed and stable set of privacy expectations."[80] Justice Alito notes that in precomputer days, the police had the time and resources to track only persons of exceptional interest to the police. He seems to accord much importance in the belief that the hypothetical reasonable person would be surprised to learn that the police would be tracking their every movement for a month-long period—an act beyond society's expectations.

Justice Sotomayor's Concurrence: The Broadest Reading of the Fourth Amendment

As far as Fourth Amendment rights are concerned, Justice Sotomayor provided the broadest interpretation in *Jones* by joining the majority's trespass approach, openly supporting Justice Alito's privacy-based approach,[81] and putting into question the continuing viability of the third-party doctrine—a theory many believe creates the largest gap in privacy protection, especially in the realm of technology.

Whereas it is unclear whether Justices Alito, Breyer, Kagan, and Ginsburg support the mosaic theory, Justice Sotomayor maintained that this theory should directly guide the Court's determination of a person's privacy expectations in their public movements.[82] She noted that "GPS monitoring generates a precise, comprehensive record of a person's public movements that reflects a wealth of detail about her familial, political, professional, religious, and sexual associations."[83] As part and parcel of the mosaic theory, she contended that an individual's awareness that the government may be constantly watching can chill one's freedom of speech and association under the First Amendment.[84] Although the police might obtain the same evidence through traditional surveillance, there is something about the technology that troubled Justice Sotomayor. She seemed concerned that there will no longer be a logistical barrier between the government and the people. Police now have access to a cheap technology that can produce a significant amount of data. The Court must consider this a search—presumably requiring a warrant—to provide adequate oversight over the executive branch.[85] This idea seems to coincide with Justice Jackson's well-worn saying that courts prefer that searches be overseen by a "neutral and detached magistrate instead of being judged by the officer engaged in the often competitive enterprise of ferreting out crime."[86]

Additionally, Justice Sotomayor called for a reexamination of the third-party doctrine. This doctrine supposes that any information a person voluntarily conveys to a third party is no longer entitled to Fourth Amendment protection, as the person cannot have a reasonable expectation that the third party will guard the privacy in that information.[87] This rule has been used to justify access to bank records,[88] the telephone numbers a person dials,[89] electric billing records,[90] and cell phone billing records.[91] Some argue that when individuals give documents to a third party, usually in a commercial transaction, they consent to the release of such information to the government,[92] or at a minimum assume the risk that the person trusted with the information would hand it over.[93] Justice Sotomayor suggests that perhaps this theory should not be permitted to reach its logical extent in the digital age, in which people convey a wealth of personal information to third parties.[94] She contends that the Fourth Amendment rules should not require a person to keep secret any information the person does not want the government to obtain. In the end, she leaves it to another day to reevaluate the third-party doctrine in an age where most private information is handed over in the course of commercial transactions. In the meantime, Justice Sotomayor believed the physical intrusion theory was enough to resolve the case.[95]

WARRANT REQUIREMENT AFTER JONES

All nine Justices agreed that tracking a person for four months is a constitutional search. Where there is little agreement among Court observers, though, is what level of suspicion is required to conduct GPS monitoring or whether a warrant is required.[96] Because the government failed to argue that a warrant was not required or that something less than probable cause would be enough to conduct this surveillance, the Court considered the arguments forfeited.[97] Thus, to determine if a warrant or something less will be required in future cases, general Fourth Amendment principles must suffice until the courts provide further guidance.

The "ultimate touchstone" of the Fourth Amendment is reasonableness, as required by the history and text of the prohibition against "unreasonable searches and seizures."[98] That is to say, once a court determines a *search* has occurred, it must then inquiry whether it was reasonable. In most instances, the Supreme Court has required the government to obtain a warrant based upon probable cause for a search to be considered reasonable.[99] A review of the cases, however, shows that this rule is not ironclad, and that the exceptions are commonplace.[100]

Some commentators argue that the automobile exception could apply to the use of a GPS tracking device.[101] The automobile exception—one of the warrantless search exceptions—evolved from the exigency requirement.[102] It was first formulated in the 1925 case of *Carroll v. United States*, in which the Court permitted the police, who had probable cause to suspect that the defendant's car was carrying bootlegged liquor, to conduct a warrantless vehicle search.[103] The Court noted that it was not practicable to obtain a warrant for evidence secreted on a "ship, motor boat, wagon or automobile" because the vehicle can be "quickly moved out of the locality or jurisdiction."[104] In later cases, the Court developed a second rationale for the automobile exception, reasoning that drivers have a diminished expectation of privacy when in their vehicles.[105] This is based on the notion that cars travel on public thoroughfares where the driver and occupants are in plain view of the public.[106] Further, cars and drivers alike are subject to extensive government regulation,[107] and vehicles must undergo periodic inspections.[108]

As noted in *Carroll*, because a vehicle can be moved quickly from the jurisdiction, requiring a warrant to attach a GPS device may not be feasible.[109] Also, tracking someone's public movements may not be as invasive as searching through a person's belongings as is currently permitted under the traditional automobile exception.[110] On the reverse side, police will generally know in advance when they intend to use a GPS device, thereby negating the presumed exigency that is linked with cars. A court could hold that warrants are generally required for GPS devices, unless a true exigency existed beyond that presumed in general automobile cases, for example, in a case of kidnapping or a fleeing suspect.

Additionally, some commentators believe that the general reasonableness standard may apply, vitiating a need for a warrant.[111] These theories suppose that the intrusion on the individual is minimal and the government interest significant. In line with this reasoning, one observer posited that a *Terry*-type standard would be sufficient—that is, that the police must have reasonable suspicion to conduct a search, but need neither probable cause nor a warrant.[112] A court would review the reasonableness after the fact, unlike warrants, where the review comes before the search.

CONCLUSION

Nine Justices are seemingly in agreement that, based on the facts of *Jones*, the attachment of a GPS device to the bottom of Jones's car and tracking him for a month-long period was a constitutional search. Presented with a different set of facts, the Court's unanimity may disintegrate. For instance, if the police need not attach the device, but it is preinstalled, for example, in a cell phone or a navigation system in a car, the outcome may differ. Further, even though this surveillance was considered a search, the Court gave no guidance on whether a warrant is required or what quantum of suspicion is enough to use GPS monitoring.

That said, it is within the power of Congress or state legislatures to propose their own requirements. The federal Constitution sets the minimum constitutional standard. Legislatures (state or federal) may create more protection of privacy and property. Congress has done this on several occasions, most notably in the field of communications with the wiretap statutes.[113] When technology is in flux, one may argue that the institutional capabilities of a legislature may be the better venue to develop these rules.[114] Justice Alito suggested this approach in his *Jones* concurrence: "In circumstances involving dramatic technological change, the best solution to privacy concerns may be legislative. A legislative body is well situated to gauge changing public attitudes, to draw detailed lines, and to balance privacy and public safety in a comprehensive way."[115]

There has been legislative activity in recent Congresses to update privacy laws to cover new technologies such as GPS. Senator Leahy has introduced the Electronic Communications Privacy Act Amendments Act of 2011 (S. 1011), which would prohibit the government from accessing or using a device to acquire geolocation information, unless it obtains a warrant based upon probable cause or a court order under Title I or Title IV of the Foreign Intelligence Surveillance Act (FISA) of 1978.[116] Similarly, Senator Ron Wyden and Representative Jason Chaffetz have introduced identical legislation, S. 1212 and H.R. 2168, entitled the Geolocational Privacy and Surveillance Act, or GPS bill, which would make it unlawful for law enforcement to intercept or use a person's location unless they obtained a warrant based upon probable cause or one of the limited exceptions applied.[117]

With each advance in technology, the courts and Congress are asked to balance a host of competing interests including privacy, property, technology, and the needs of law enforcement. It will take future cases and statutes to better delineate a proper balance.

End Notes

[1] U.S. Const. amend. IV.

[2] United States v. Jones, 132 S. Ct. 945, 948 (2012).

[3] GPS is a network of 24 government satellites that constantly send out radio signals and allow a receiver on Earth to determine its position. Aaron Renenger, *Satellite Tracking and the Right to Privacy*, 53 HASTINGS L. J. 549, 550 (2002).

[4] John Ganz, *It's Already Public: Why Federal Officers Should Not Need Warrants to Use GPS Vehicle Tracking Devices*, 95 CRIM. L. & CRIMINOLOGY 1325, 1330 (2005).

[5] United States v. Knotts, 460 U.S. 276, 278-79 (1983) (holding that use of tracking device while suspect was on public thoroughfares was not a violation of the Fourth Amendment as he had no reasonable expectation of privacy in his public movements); United States v. Karo, 468 U.S. 705, 718 (1984) (holding that use of tracking of device while in private home was a violation of the Fourth Amendment).

[6] This reasonable expectation of privacy test was formulated by Justice Harlan in his *Katz* concurrence. Katz v. United States, 389 U.S. 347, 361 (1967) (Harlan, J., concurring).

[7] *Jones*, 132 S. Ct. at 952.

[8] *Id.* at 951 n.5.

[9] *Id.* at 958 (Alito, J., concurring).

[10] *Id.* at 957 (Sotomayor, J., concurring).

[11] *Id.* at 948.

[12] A pen register is a device that determines the outgoing telephone numbers dialed from a telephone. 18 U.S.C. § 3127(3).

[13] Since the device was attached one day late and in the wrong jurisdiction, the installation was considered warrantless.

[14] *Id.*

[15] *Id.* at 948-49.

[16] United States v. Jones, 451 F. Supp. 2d 71, 88 (D. D.C. 2006).

[17] *Jones*, 132 S. Ct. at 949.

[18] United States v. Maynard, 615 F.3d 544, 555 (D.C. Cir. 2010). Because Jones's case was consolidated with other codefendants on appeal, it was entitled *United States v. Maynard* before the D.C. Circuit Court of Appeals. It was subsequently changed back to *United States v. Jones* when reviewed by the Supreme Court.

[19] Katz v. United States, 389 U.S. 347, 361 (1967) (Harlan, J., concurring).

[20] *See* Kyllo v. United States, 533 U.S. 27, 32 (2001) ("In assessing when a search is not a search, we have applied somewhat in reverse the principle first enunciated in *Katz v. United States*, 389 U.S. 347, 19 L. Ed. 2d 576, 88 S. Ct. 507 (1967)); California v. Ciraolo, 476 U.S. 207, 215 (1986) ("The touchstone of Fourth Amendment analysis is whether a person has a 'constitutionally protected reasonable expectation of privacy.' Katz v. United States, 389 U.S. 347, 360 (1967) (Harlan, J., concurring).")).

[21] The majority consisted of Chief Justice Roberts, and Justices Thomas, Kennedy, and Sotomayor. In addition to joining the majority opinion, Justice Sotomayor also wrote a concurring opinion explored below.

[22] *Jones*, 132 S. Ct. at 949.

[23] U.S. CONST. amend IV.

[24] *Jones*, 132 S. Ct. at 949.

[25] *Id.* at 950.

> The Government contends that the Harlan standard shows that no search occurred here, since Jones had no "reasonable expectation of privacy" in the area of the Jeep accessed by Government agents (its underbody) and in the locations of the Jeep on the public roads, which were visible to all. But we need not address the Government's contentions, because Jones's Fourth Amendment rights do not rise or fall with the Katz formulation. At bottom, we must "assur[e] preservation of that degree of privacy against government that existed when the Fourth Amendment was adopted."
>
> *Id.*

[26] *Id.* at 958 (Alito, J., concurring).

[27] *Id.*

[28] Entick v. Carrington, 95 Eng. Rep. 807 (C.P. 1765); *see* Ricardo J. Bascaus, *Property and Probable Cause: The Fourth Amendment's Principled Protection of Privacy*, 60 RUTGERS L. REV. 575, 581-82 (2008).

[29] Entick v. Carrington, 95 Eng. Rep. 807 (C.P. 1765).

[30] *See* Amil Akir, *Fourth Amendment First Principles*, 107 HARV. L. REV. 757, 767 (1994).

[31] *Jones*, 132 S. Ct. at 950.

[32] Olmstead v. United States, 277 U.S. 438, 456-57 (1928).

[33] *Id.* at 466.

[34] *Id.*

[35] Warden, Maryland Penitentiary v. Hayden, 387 U.S. 294, 304 (1967) ("We have recognized that the principal object of the Fourth Amendment is the protection of privacy rather than

property, and have increasingly discarded fictional and procedural barriers rested on property concepts.").

[36] Katz v. United States, 389 U.S. 347, 359 (1967).

[37] *Id.* at 351, 360 (Harlan, J., concurring).

[38] Soldal v. County of Cook, 506 U.S. 56 (1992).

[39] *Id.* at 58.

[40] Soldal v. County of Cook, 942 F.2d 1073, 1078 (7th Cir. 1991).

[41] *Id.*

[42] *Soldal*, 506 U.S. at 65.

[43] *Id.* at 64.

[44] *Id.* at 64 n.7.

[45] *Jones*, 132 S. Ct. at 950-951.

[46] *Id.* at 951 n.5. It is not clear from the majority opinion whether a mere attempt to obtain information is enough, or if the attempt must be successful. In one phrasing the Court requires "installation of a GPS device on a target's vehicle, and its *use* of that device....," *Id.* at 949 (emphasis added), and in another it requires a trespass plus "an *attempt* to find or to obtain information." *Id.* at 951 n.5 (emphasis added). A reasonable interpretation is that an attempt is enough: if the police were to come into a person's home looking for evidence, but found nothing, this would probably qualify under the majority's approach.

[47] *Id.* at 953 n.8.

[48] *Id.* at 953.

[49] The importance of these concurrences was noted by an FBI attorney: "[E]ven though its not technically holding, we have to anticipate how it's going to go down the road." Julia Angwin, *FBI Turns Off Thousands of GPS Devices After Supreme Court Ruling* (Feb. 25, 2012, 3:36 PM), http://blogs.

[50] Jones, 132 S. Ct. at 854 (Sotomayor, J., concurring); 132 S. Ct. at 957 (Alito, J., concurring).

[51] United States v. Hanna, No. 11-20678-CR, 2012 WL 279435, at *3 (S.D. Fla. Jan. 3, 2012) (analyzing the issue of Fourth Amendment standing under both the trespass theory and *Katz*'s privacy test); United States v. Bradshaw, No. 1:11-CR-257, 2012 WL 774964 (N.D. Ohio Mar. 8, 2012) (noting that the *Jones* majority did not adopt the mosaic theory); State v. Zahn, No. 25584, 2012 WL 862707 (S.D. Mar. 14, 2012) (holding that both the trespass approach and the mosaic theory can apply to GPS tracking).

[52] This dialogue between concurring justices and those they are trying to persuade lies at the heart of the common law system—a case-by-case discussion between judges, lawyers, and the public about the progression of the law. RICHARD A. POSNER, THE FEDERAL COURTS: CRISIS AND REFORM 236 (1985).

[53] Igor Kirman, *Standing Apart to Be a Part: The Precedential Value of Supreme Court Concurring Opinions*, 95 COLUM L. REV. 2083, 2096-2101 (1995) (explaining that some courts will presume precedential value in a concurring opinion while others will presume no precedential value).

[54] Lewis A. Kornhauser & Lawrence G. Sager, *The One and the Many: Adjudication in Collegial Courts*, 81 CAL. L. REV. 1 (1993).

[55] Kirman, *supra* note 53, 2119.

[56] Scott C. Idleman, *A Prudential Theory of Judicial Candor*, 73 TEX. L. REV. 1307, 1371 (1995).

[57] Mark Tushnet, *Themes in Warren Court Biographies*, 70 N.Y.U. L. REV. 748, 763 (1995).

[58] *Jones*, 132 S. Ct. at 957 (Alito, J., concurring) Justice Alito contended that the Court melded the two distinct acts of *search* and *seizure* into one to develop its holding; that this approach

is merely a return to the much-criticized *Olmstead*, when property controlled; that there are no 18th century analogs to GPS; and that the attachment would not suffice even under common tort law. *Id.*

[59] *Jones*, 132 S. Ct. at 958-59 (Alito, J., concurring).

[60] United States v. Maynard, 615 F.3d 544, 558 (D.C. Cir. 2010).

[61] *Id.* at 558.

[62] *Id.*

[63] *Id.* at 561-62.

[64] Cen. Int. Agency v. Sims, 471 U.S. 159, 178 (1985).

[65] *Id.* at 178.

[66] United States v. Knotts, 460 U.S. 276, 281 (1983).

[67] *Knotts*, 460 U.S. at 281.

[68] *Id.* at 283.

[69] *Id.* This phrase was dicta, meaning it was not essential to the case; thus it is persuasive, but not binding on lower courts.

[70] *Maynard*, 615 F.3d at 556.

[71] *Id.* at 558.

[72] *Jones*, 132 S. Ct. at 951. The Court did not repudiate the mosaic theory, but instead did not reach the question of whether this privacy-based theory would apply; the property-based approach was sufficient to resolve the case.

[73] *Id.* at 958 (Alito, J., concurring). Query whether the reasonable expectation of privacy test is designed to test what privacy the average person would expect. *See* Orin Kerr, *The Fourth Amendment and New Technologies*, 102 MICH. L. REV. 801, 838 (2004) ("A 'reasonable expectation of privacy' has not been equated with the expectation of privacy of a reasonable person; rather, it has been used as a term of art based heavily on property law principles.").

[74] *Jones*, 132 S. Ct. at 964 (Alito, J., concurring).

[75] *Id.*

[76] *Id.*

[77] The mosaic theory need not be cabined to only the GPS tracking scenario. It could apply in other contexts such as smart electric meters, Internet searches, or any other activity in which surveillance of activity over a long period of time can be aggregated to produce an in-depth look into the subject's daily activities, belief systems, etc. CRS Report R42338, *Smart Meter Data: Privacy and Cybersecurity*, by Brandon J. Murrill, Edward C. Liu, and Richard M. Thompson II.

[78] Orin Kerr, *What's the Status of the Mosaic Theory After Jones?*, THE VOLOKH CONSPIRACY (Jan. 23, 2012, 1:59 PM), http://volokh.com/2012/01/23/whats-the-status-of-the-mosaic

[79] Orin S. Kerr, *Four Models of Fourth Amendment Protection*, 60 STAN. L. REV. 503, 509 (2007).

[80] *Jones*, 132 S. Ct. at 962 (Alito, J., concurring).

[81] Although she could not join his opinion, Justice Sotomayor clearly supported Justice Alito's reasoning. *Jones*, 132 S. Ct. at 956 (Sotomayor, J., concurring) ("As Justice Alito incisively observes ...."; "I agree with Justice Alito....").

[82] *Id.*

[83] *Id.*

[84] *Id.*

[85] *Id.*

[86] Johnson v. United States, 333 U.S. 10, 14 (1948).

[87] United States v. Miller, 425 U.S. 435, 443 (1976). "The Fourth Amendment does not prohibit the obtaining of information revealed to a third party and conveyed by him to Government authorities, even if the information is revealed on the assumption that it will be used only for a limited purpose and the confidence placed in the third party will not be betrayed." *Id.*

[88] *Miller*, 425 U.S. at 435.

[89] Smith v. Maryland, 442 U.S. 735 (1979).

[90] United States v. McIntyre, 646 F.3d 1107 (8th Cir. 2011).

[91] United States v. Hynson, No. 05-576, 2007 WL 2692327, at *6 (E.D. Pa. Sept. 11, 2007).

[92] *See* Orin S. Kerr, *The Case for a Third-Party Doctrine*, 107 MICH. L. REV. 561, 565 (2009).

[93] *Smith*, 442 U.S. at 744 ("Because the depositor [in *Miller*] 'assumed the risk' of disclosure, the Court held that it would be unreasonable for him to expect his financial records to remain private.").

[94] *Jones*, 132 S. Ct. at 957 (Sotomayor, J., concurring).

[95] *Id.*

[96] *See* Peter Swire, *A Reasonableness Approach to Searches After the Jones GPS Tracking Case*, 64 STAN. L. REV. ONLINE 57 (2012); Daniel J. Solove, *United States v. Jones and the Future of Privacy Law: The Potential Far-Reaching Implications of the GPS Surveillance Case*, 90 CRIM. L. REPER. 632 (2012); Tom Goldstein, Why Jones is still less of a pro-privacy decision than most thought, SCOTUSblog (Jan. 30, 2012, 10:53 AM), http://www.scotusblog.com/2012/01/why-jones-is-still-less-of-a-pro-privacy-decision-than-most-thought/.

[97] *Jones*, 132 S. Ct. at 954.

[98] Brigham City v. Stuart, 547 U.S. 398, 403 (2006); Nat'l Treasury Employees Union v. Von Raab, 489 U.S. 656, 665 (1989); California v. Acevedo, 500 U.S. 565, 581 (1991) (Scalia, J., concurring in the judgment).

[99] Mincey v. Arizona, 437 U.S. 385, 390 (1978) (quoting Katz v. United States, 389 U.S. 347, 357 (1967)).

[100] The Court often states that "[t]he Fourth Amendment proscribes all unreasonable searches and seizures, and it is a cardinal principle that 'searches conducted outside the judicial process, without prior approval by judge or magistrate, are *per se* unreasonable under the Fourth Amendment—subject only to a few specifically established and well-delineated exceptions.'" United States v. Ross, 456 U.S. 798, 825 (1982) (quoting Katz v. United States, 389 U.S. 347, 357 (1967)). One scholar aptly commented on this rule:

In fact, these exceptions are neither few nor well-delineated. There are over twenty exceptions to the probable cause or the warrant requirement or both. They include searches incident to arrest (exceptions to both); automobile searches (exception to warrant requirement); border searches (both); searches near the border (warrant and sometimes both); administrative searches (probable cause exception); administrative searches of regulated businesses (warrant); stop and frisk (both); plain view, open field seizures and prison "shakedowns" (both, because they are not covered by the fourth amendment at all); exigent circumstances (warrant); search of a person in custody (both); search incident to nonarrest when there is probable cause to arrest (both); fire investigations (warrant); warrantless entry following arrest elsewhere (warrant); boat boarding for document checks (both); consent searches (both); welfare searches (both, because not a "search"); inventory searches (both); driver's license and vehicle registration checks (both); airport searches (both); searches at courthouse doors (both); the new "school search" (both); and finally the standing doctrine which, while not strictly an exception to fourth amendment requirements, has that effect by causing the courts to ignore fourth amendment violations.

Craig M. Bradley, *Two Models of the Fourth Amendments*, 83 MICH. L. REV. 1468, 1473-74 (1985) (internal citations omitted).

[101] Goldstein, *supra* note 96.

[102] Carol A. Chase, *Privacy Takes a Back Seat: Putting the Automobile Exception Back on Track after Several Wrong Turns*, 41 B.C. L. REV. 71, 75 (1999).

[103] Carroll v. United States, 267 U.S. 132 (1925).

[104] *Id.* at 153.

[105] United States v. Chadwick, 433 U.S. 1, 12-13 (1977).

[106] Cardwell v. Lewis, 417 U.S. 583, 590 (1974).

[107] Cady v. Dombrowski, 413 U.S. 433, 441 (1973) ("All States require vehicles to be registered and operators to be licensed. States and localities have enacted extensive and detailed codes regulating the condition and manner in which motor vehicles may be operated on public streets and highways.").

[108] South Dakota v. Opperman, 428 U.S. 364, 367-8 (1976).

[109] *See* Orin Kerr, Jones, *the Automobile Exception, and the Warrant Requirement*, THE VOLOKH CONSPIRACY (Feb. 2, 2012 12:45 AM), http://volokh.com/2012/02/02/jones-the-automobile-exception-and-the-warrant-requirement/.

[110] *Id.*

[111] *See* Swire, *supra* note 96; Goldstein, *supra* note 96.

[112] Swire, *supra* note 96.

[113] Kerr, *supra* note 73, at 839. For an in-depth look at the statutory regulation of communication surveillance, see CRS Report R41733, *Privacy: An Overview of the Electronic Communications Privacy Act*, by Charles Doyle.

[114] *Id.* at 857.

The difference favors legislatures when technology is in flux because the privacy implications of particular rules can fluctuate as technology advances. To ensure that the law maintains its intended balance, it needs mechanisms that can adapt to technological change. Legislatures are up to the task; courts generally are not. Legislatures can experiment with different rules and make frequent amendments; they can place restrictions on both public and private actors; and they can even "sunset" rules so that they apply only for a particular period of time. The courts cannot. As a result, Fourth Amendment rules will tend to lack the flexibility that a regulatory response to new technologies may require.... The statutory framework that governs Internet privacy demonstrates the flexibility and creative potential of legislative approaches.

Id. at 871.

[115] *Jones*, 132 S. Ct. at 964 (Alito, J., concurring).

[116] S. 1011, 112th Cong., 1st Sess. (2011).

[117] S. 1212, H.R. 2168, 112th Cong., 1st Sess. (2011).

In: Legalities of GPS and Cell Phone Surveillance ISBN: 978-1-62257-026-3
Editors: E. Johnson and M. Rodriguez

Chapter 4

DECISION OF THE SUPREME COURT OF THE UNITED STATES IN THE CASE OF UNITED STATES V. JONES*

Supreme Court of the United States

Certiorari to the United States Court of Appeals for the District of Columbia Circuit

Argued November 8, 2011—Decided January 23, 2012

The Government obtained a search warrant permitting it to install a Global-Positioning-System (GPS) tracking device on a vehicle registered to respondent Jones's wife. The warrant authorized installation in the District of Columbia and within 10 days, but agents in-stalled the device on the 11th day and in Maryland. The Government then tracked the vehicle's movements for 28 days. It subsequently secured an indictment of Jones and others on drug trafficking conspiracy charges. The District Court suppressed the GPS data obtained while the vehicle was parked at Jones's residence, but held the remaining data admissible because Jones had no reasonable expectation of privacy when the vehicle was on public streets. Jones was convicted. The D. C. Circuit reversed, concluding that admission of the evidence obtained by warrantless use of the GPS device violated the Fourth Amendment.

---

* This is an edited, reformatted and augmented version of the Supreme Court of the United States, No. 10–1259., dated January 23, 2012.

Held: The Government's attachment of the GPS device to the vehicle, and its use of that device to monitor the vehicle's movements, constitutes a search under the Fourth Amendment. Pp. 3–12.

(a) The Fourth Amendment protects the "right of the people to be secure in their persons, houses, papers, and effects, against unreasonable searches and seizures." Here, the Government's physical intrusion on an "effect" for the purpose of obtaining information constitutes a "search." This type of encroachment on an area enumerated in the Amendment would have been considered a search within the meaning of the Amendment at the time it was adopted. Pp. 3–4.

(b) This conclusion is consistent with this Court's Fourth Amendment jurisprudence, which until the latter half of the 20th century was tied to common-law trespass. Later cases, which have deviated from that exclusively property-based approach, have applied the analysis of Justice Harlan's concurrence in *Katz* v. *United States*, 389 U. S. 347, which said that the Fourth Amendment protects a person's "reasonable expectation of privacy," *id.*, at 360. Here, the Court need not address the Government's contention that Jones had no "reasonable expectation of privacy," because Jones's Fourth Amendment rights do not rise or fall with the *Katz* formulation. At bottom, the Court must "assur[e] preservation of that degree of privacy against government that existed when the Fourth Amendment was adopted." *Kyllo* v. *United States*, 533 U. S. 27, 34. *Katz* did not repudiate the understanding that the Fourth Amendment embodies a particular concern for government trespass upon the areas it enumerates. The *Katz* reasonable-expectation-of-privacy test has been added to, butnot substituted for, the common-law trespassory test. See *Alderman* v. *United States*, 394 U. S. 165, 176; *Soldal* v. *Cook County*, 506 U. S. 56, 64. *United States* v. *Knotts*, 460 U. S. 276, and *United States* v. *Karo*, 468 U. S. 705—post-*Katz* cases rejecting Fourth Amendment challenges to "beepers," electronic tracking devices representing another form of electronic monitoring—do not foreclose the conclusion that a search occurred here. *New York* v. *Class*, 475 U. S. 106, and *Oliver* v. *United States*, 466 U. S. 170, also do not support the Government's position. Pp. 4–12.

(c) The Government's alternative argument—that if the attach-ment and use of the device was a search, it was a reasonable one—is forfeited because it was not raised below. P. 12. 615 F. 3d 544, affirmed.

Scalia, J., delivered the opinion of the Court, in which Roberts, C. J., and Kennedy, Thomas, and Sotomayor, JJ., joined. Sotomayor, J., filed a concurring opinion. Alito, J., filed an opinion concurring in the judgment, in which Ginsburg, Breyer, and Kagan, JJ., joined.

Opinion of the Court

United States, Petitioner v. Antoine Jones
On Writ of Certiorari to the United States Court of Appeals for the District of Columbia Circuit
[January 23, 2012]

Justice Scalia delivered the opinion of the Court.

We decide whether the attachment of a Global-Positioning-System (GPS) tracking device to an individual's vehicle, and subsequent use of that device to monitor the vehicle's movements on public streets, constitutes a search or seizure within the meaning of the Fourth Amendment.

I

In 2004 respondent Antoine Jones, owner and operator of a nightclub in the District of Columbia, came under suspicion of trafficking in narcotics and was made the target of an investigation by a joint FBI and Metropolitan Police Department task force. Officers employed various investigative techniques, including visual surveillance of the nightclub, installation of a camera focused on the front door of the club, and a pen register and wiretap covering Jones's cellular phone.

Based in part on information gathered from these sources, in 2005 the Government applied to the United States District Court for the District of Columbia for a warrant authorizing the use of an electronic tracking device on the Jeep Grand Cherokee registered to Jones's wife. A warrant issued, authorizing installation of the device in the District of Columbia and within 10 days.

On the 11th day, and not in the District of Columbia but in Maryland,[1] agents installed a GPS tracking device on the undercarriage of the Jeep while it was parked in a public parking lot. Over the next 28 days, the Government used the device to track the vehicle's movements, and once had to replace the device's battery when the vehicle was parked in a different public lot in

Maryland. By means of signals from multiple satellites, the device established the vehicle's location within 50 to 100 feet, and communicated that location by cellular phone to a Government computer. It relayed more than 2,000 pages of data over the 4-week period.

The Government ultimately obtained a multiple-count indictment charging Jones and several alleged co-conspirators with, as relevant here, conspiracy to istribute and possess with intent to distribute five kilograms or more of cocaine and 50 grams or more of cocaine base, in violation of 21 U. S. C. §§841 and 846. Before trial, Jones filed a motion to suppress evidence obtained through the GPS device. The District Court granted the motion only in part, suppressing the data obtained while the vehicle was parked in the garage adjoining Jones's residence. 451 F. Supp. 2d 71, 88 (2006). It held the remaining data admissible, because "'[a] person traveling in an automobile on public thoroughfares has no reasonable expectation of privacy in his movements from one place to another.' " *Ibid.* (quoting *United States* v. *Knotts*, 460 U. S. 276, 281 (1983)). Jones's trial in October 2006 produced a hung jury on the conspiracy count.

In March 2007, a grand jury returned another indictment, charging Jones and others with the same conspiracy. The Government introduced at trial the same GPS-derived locational data admitted in the first trial, which connected Jones to the alleged conspirators' stash house that contained $850,000 in cash, 97 kilograms of cocaine, and 1 kilogram of cocaine base. The jury returned a guilty verdict, and the District Court sentenced Jones to life imprisonment.

The United States Court of Appeals for the District ofColumbia Circuit reversed the conviction because of ad-mission of the evidence obtained by warrantless use of the GPS device which, it said, violated the Fourth Amendment. *United States* v. *Maynard*, 615 F. 3d 544 (2010).The D. C. Circuit denied the Government's petition for rehearing en banc, with four judges dissenting. 625 F. 3d 766 (2010). We granted certiorari, 564 U. S. ___ (2011).

II

A

The Fourth Amendment provides in relevant part that "[t]he right of the people to be secure in their persons, houses, papers, and effects, against unreasonable searches and seizures, shall not be violated." It is beyond dispute that a vehicle is an "effect" as that term is used in the Amendment. *United States* v. *Chadwick*, 433 U. S. 1, 12 (1977). We hold that the Government's installation of a GPS device on a target's vehicle,[2] and its use of that device to monitor the vehicle's movements, constitutes a "search."

It is important to be clear about what occurred in this case: The Government physically occupied private property for the purpose of obtaining information. We have no doubt that such a physical intrusion would have been considered a "search" within the meaning of the Fourth Amendment when it was adopted. *Entick* v. *Carrington*, 95 Eng. Rep. 807 (C. P. 1765), is a "case we have described as a 'monument of English freedom' 'undoubtedly familiar' to 'every American statesman' at the time the Constitution was adopted, and considered to be 'the true and ultimate expression of constitutional law'" with regard to search and seizure. *Brower* v. *County of Inyo*, 489 U. S. 593, 596 (1989) (quoting *Boyd* v. *United States*, 116 U. S. 616, 626 (1886)). In that case, Lord Camden expressed in plain terms the significance of property rights in search-and-seizure analysis:

> "[O]ur law holds the property of every man so sacred, that no man can set his foot upon his neighbour's close without his leave; if he does he is a trespasser, though he does no damage at all; if he will tread upon his neighbour's ground, he must justify it by law." *Entick, supra,* at 817.

The text of the Fourth Amendment reflects its close connection to property, since otherwise it would have referred simply to "the right of the people to be secure against unreasonable searches and seizures"; the phrase "in their persons, houses, papers, and effects" would have been superfluous.

Consistent with this understanding, our Fourth Amendment jurisprudence was tied to common-law trespass, at least until the latter half of the 20th century. *Kyllo* v. *United States*, 533 U. S. 27, 31 (2001); Kerr, The Fourth Amendment and New Technologies: Constitutional Myths and the Case for Caution, 102 Mich. L. Rev. 801, 816 (2004). Thus, in *Olmstead* v. *United States*, 277 U. S. 438 (1928), we held that wiretaps attached to telephone wires on the public streets did not constitute a Fourth Amendment search because "[t]here was no entry of the houses or offices of the defendants," *id.*, at 464.

Our later cases, of course, have deviated from that exclusively property-based approach. In *Katz* v. *United States*, 389 U. S. 347, 351 (1967), we said that "the Fourth Amendment protects people, not places," and found a violation in attachment of an eavesdropping device to a public telephone booth. Our later cases have applied the analysis of Justice Harlan's concurrence in that case, which said that a violation occurs when government officers violate a person's "reasonable expectation of privacy," *id.*, at 360. See, *e.g.*, *Bond* v. *United States*, 529 U. S. 334 (2000); *California* v. *Ciraolo*, 476 U. S. 207 (1986); *Smith* v. *Maryland*, 442 U. S. 735 (1979).

The Government contends that the Harlan standard shows that no search occurred here, since Jones had no "reasonable expectation of privacy" in the area of the Jeep accessed by Government agents (its underbody) and in the locations of the Jeep on the public roads, which were visible to all. But we need not address the Government's contentions, because Jones's Fourth Amendment rights do not rise or fall with the *Katz* formulation. At bottom, we must "assur[e] preservation of that degree of privacy against government that existed when the Fourth Amendment was adopted." *Kyllo*, *supra*, at 34. As explained, for most of our history the Fourth Amendment was understood to embody a particular concern for government trespass upon the areas ("persons, houses, papers, and effects") it enumerates.[3] *Katz* did not repudiate that understanding. Less than two years later the Court upheld defendants' contention that the Government could not introduce against them conversations between *other* people obtained by warrantless placement of electronic surveillance devices in their homes. The opinion rejected the dissent's contention that there was no Fourth Amendment violation "unless the conversational privacy of the homeowner himself is invaded."[4] *Alderman* v. *United States*, 394 U. S. 165, 176 (1969). "[W]e [do not] believe that *Katz*, by holding that the Fourth Amendment protects persons and their private conversations, was intended to withdraw any of the protection which the Amendment extends to the home . . . ." *Id.*, at 180.

More recently, in *Soldal* v. *Cook County*, 506 U. S. 56 (1992), the Court unanimously rejected the argument that although a "seizure" had occurred "in a 'technical' sense" when a trailer home was forcibly removed, *id.*, at 62, no Fourth Amendment violation occurred because law enforcement had not "invade[d] the [individuals'] privacy," *id.*, at 60. *Katz*, the Court explained, established that "property rights are not the sole measure of Fourth Amendment violations," but did not "snuf[f] out the previously recognized protection for property." 506 U. S., at 64. As Justice Brennan explained in his concurrence in *Knotts*, *Katz* did not erode the principle "that, when the Government *does* engage in physical intrusion of a constitutionally protected area in order to obtain information, that intrusion may constitute a violation of the Fourth Amendment." 460 U. S., at 286 (opinion concurring in judgment). We have embodied that preservation of past rights in our very definition of "reasonable expectation of privacy" which we have said to be an expectation "that has a source outside of the Fourth Amendment, either by reference to concepts of real or personal property law or to understandings that are recognized and permitted by society." *Minnesota* v. *Carter*, 525 U. S. 83, 88 (1998) (internal quotation marks omitted). *Katz* did not narrow the Fourth Amendment's scope.[5]

The Government contends that several of our post-*Katz* cases foreclose the conclusion that what occurred here constituted a search. It relies principally on two cases in which we rejected Fourth Amendment challenges to "beepers," electronic tracking devices that represent an-other form of electronic monitoring. The first case, *Knotts*, upheld against Fourth Amendment challenge the use of a "beeper" that had been placed in a container of chloroform, allowing law enforcement to monitor the location of the container. 460 U. S., at 278. We said that there had been no infringement of Knotts' reasonable expectation of privacy since the information obtained—the location of the automobile carrying the container on public roads, and the location of the off-loaded container in open fields near Knotts' cabin—had been voluntarily conveyed to the public.[6] *Id.*, at 281–282. But as we have discussed, the *Katz* reasonable-expectation-of-privacy test has been *added to*, not *substituted for*, the common-law trespassory test. The holding in *Knotts* addressed only the former, since the latter was not at issue. The beeper had been placed in the container before it came into Knotts' possession, with the consent of the then-owner. 460 U. S., at 278. Knotts did not challenge that installation, and we specifically declined to consider its effect on the Fourth Amendment analysis. *Id.*, at 279, n. *Knotts* would be relevant, per-haps, if the Government were making the argument that what would otherwise be an unconstitutional search is not such where it produces only public information. The Government does not make that argument, and we know of no case that would support it.

The second "beeper" case, *United States* v. *Karo*, 468 U. S. 705 (1984), does not suggest a different conclusion. There we addressed the question left open by *Knotts*, whether the installation of a beeper in a container amounted to a search or seizure. 468 U. S., at 713. As in *Knotts*, at the time the beeper was installed the container belonged to a third party, and it did not come into possession of the defendant until later. 468 U. S., at 708. Thus, the specific question we considered was whether the installation "*with the consent of the original owner* constitute[d] a search or seizure . . . when the container is delivered to a buyer having no knowledge of the presence of the beeper." *Id.*, at 707 (emphasis added). We held not. The Government, we said, came into physical contact with the container only before it belonged to the defendant Karo; and the transfer of the container with the unmonitored beeper inside did not convey any information and thus did not invade Karo's privacy. See *id.*, at 712. That conclusion is perfectly consistent with the one we reach here. Karo accepted the container as it came to him, beeper and all, and was therefore not entitled to object to the beeper's presence, even though it was used to monitor the container's location. Cf. *On Lee* v. *United States*, 343 U. S. 747, 751–752 (1952) (no search or seizure where an informant, who was wearing a concealed microphone, was invited into the defendant's business). Jones, who possessed the Jeep at the time the Government trespassorily inserted the information-gathering device, is on much different footing.

The Government also points to our exposition in *New York* v. *Class*, 475 U. S. 106 (1986), that "[t]he exterior of a car . . . is thrust into the public eye, and thus to examine it does not constitute a 'search.'" *Id.*, at 114. That statement is of marginal relevance here since, as the Government acknowledges, "the officers in this case did *more* than conduct a visual inspection of respondent's vehicle," Brief for United States 41 (emphasis added). By attaching the device to the Jeep, officers encroached on a protected area. In *Class* itself we suggested that this would make a difference, for we concluded that an officer's momentary reaching into the interior of a vehicle did constitute a search.[7] 475 U. S., at 114–115.

Finally, the Government's position gains little support from our conclusion in *Oliver* v. *United States*, 466 U. S. 170 (1984), that officers' information-gathering intrusion on an "open field" did not constitute a Fourth Amendment search even though it was a trespass at common law, *id.*, at 183. Quite simply, an open field, unlike the curtilage of a home, see *United States* v. *Dunn*, 480 U. S. 294, 300 (1987), is not one of those protected areas enumerated in the Fourth Amendment. *Oliver, supra*, at 176–177. See also *Hester* v. *United States*, 265 U. S. 57, 59 (1924). The Government's physical intrusion on such an area—unlike its intrusion on the "effect" at issue here—is of no Fourth Amendment significance.[8]

B

The concurrence begins by accusing us of applying"18th-century tort law." *Post*, at 1. That is a distortion. What we apply is an 18th-century guarantee against un- reasonable searches, which we believe must provide *at a minimum* the degree of protection it afforded when it was adopted. The concurrence does not share that belief. It would apply *exclusively Katz*'s reasonable-expectation-of-privacy test, even when that eliminates rights that previously existed.

The concurrence faults our approach for "present[ing] particularly vexing problems" in cases that do not involve physical contact, such as those that involve the transmission of electronic signals. *Post*, at 9. We entirely fail to understand that point. For unlike the concurrence, which would make *Katz* the *exclusive* test, we do not make trespass the exclusive test. Situations involving merely the transmission of electronic signals without trespass would *remain* subject to *Katz* analysis.

In fact, it is the concurrence's insistence on the exclusivity of the *Katz* test that needlessly leads us into "particularly vexing problems" in the present case. This Court has to date not deviated from the understanding that mere visual observation does not constitute a search. See *Kyllo*, 533 U. S., at 31–32. We accordingly held in *Knotts* that "[a] person traveling in an automobile on public thorough-fares has no reasonable expectation of privacy in his movements from one place to another." 460 U. S., at 281. Thus, even assuming that the concurrence is correct to say that "[t]raditional surveillance" of Jones for a 4-weekperiod "would have required a large team of agents, multiple vehicles, and perhaps aerial assistance," *post*, at 12, our cases suggest that such visual observation is constitutionally permissible. It may be that achieving the same result through electronic means, without an accompany-ing trespass, is an unconstitutional invasion of privacy, but the present case does not require us to answer that question.

And answering it affirmatively leads us needlessly into additional thorny problems. The concurrence posits that "relatively short-term monitoring of a person's movements on public streets" is okay, but that "the use of longer term GPS monitoring in investigations *of most offenses*" is no good. *Post*, at 13 (emphasis added). That introduces yet another novelty into our jurisprudence. There is no precedent for the proposition that whether a search has occurred depends on the nature of the crime being investigated. And even accepting that novelty, it remains unexplained why a 4-week investigation is "surely" too long and why a drug-trafficking conspiracy involving substantial amounts of cash and narcotics is not an "extra- ordinary offens[e]" which may permit longer observation. See *post*, at 13–14. What of a 2-day monitoring of a suspected purveyor of stolen electronics? Or of a 6-month monitoring of a suspected terrorist? We may have to grapple with these "vexing problems" in some future case where a classic trespassory search is not involved and resort must be had to *Katz* analysis; but there is no reason for rushing forward to resolve them here.

III

The Government argues in the alternative that even if the attachment and use of the device was a search, it was reasonable—and thus lawful—under the Fourth Amendment because "officers had reasonable suspicion, and in-deed probable cause, to believe that [Jones] was a leader in a large-scale cocaine distribution conspiracy." Brief for United States 50–51. We have no occasion to consider this argument. The Government did not raise it below, and the D. C. Circuit therefore did not address it. See 625 F. 3d, at 767 (Ginsburg, Tatel, and Griffith, JJ., concur-ring in denial of rehearing en banc). We consider the argument forfeited. See *Sprietsma* v. *Mercury Marine*, 537 U. S. 51, 56, n. 4 (2002).

The judgment of the Court of Appeals for the D. C. Circuit is affirmed.
It is so ordered.

Sotomayor, J., Concurring

I join the Court's opinion because I agree that a search within the meaning of the Fourth Amendment occurs, at a minimum, "[w]here, as here, the Government obtains information by physically intruding on a constitutionally protected area." *Ante,* at 6, n. 3. In this case, the Government installed a Global Positioning System (GPS) tracking device on respondent Antoine Jones' Jeep without a valid warrant and without Jones' consent, then used that device to monitor the Jeep's movements over the course of four weeks. The Government usurped Jones' property for the purpose of conducting surveillance on him, thereby invading privacy interests long afforded, and undoubtedly entitled to, Fourth Amendment protection. See, *e.g., Silverman* v. *United States*, 365 U. S. 505, 511– 512 (1961).

Of course, the Fourth Amendment is not concerned only with trespassory intrusions on property. See, *e.g., Kyllo* v. *United States*, 533 U. S. 27, 31–33 (2001). Rather, even in the absence of a trespass, "a Fourth Amendment search occurs when the government violates a subjective expectation of privacy that society recognizes as reasonable." *Id.,* at 33; see also *Smith* v. *Maryland*, 442 U. S. 735, 740–741 (1979); *Katz* v. *United States*, 389 U. S. 347, 361 (1967)

(Harlan, J., concurring). In *Katz*, this Court enlarged its then-prevailing focus on property rights by announcing that the reach of the Fourth Amendment does not "turn upon the presence or absence of a physical intrusion." *Id.,* at 353. As the majority's opinion makes clear, however, *Katz*'s reasonable-expectation-of-privacy test augmented, but did not displace or diminish, the common-law trespassory test that preceded it. *Ante,* at 8. Thus, "when the Government *does* engage in physical intrusion of a constitutionally protected area in order to obtain information, that intrusion may constitute a violation of the Fourth Amendment." *United States* v. *Knotts*, 460 U. S. 276, 286 (1983) (Brennan, J., concurring in judgment); see also, *e.g., Rakas* v. *Illinois*, 439 U. S. 128, 144, n. 12 (1978). JUSTICE ALITO'S approach, which discounts altogether the constitutional relevance of the Government's physical intrusion on Jones' Jeep, erodes that longstanding protection for privacy expectations inherent in items of property that people possess or control. See *post,* at 5–7 (opinion concurring in judgment). By contrast, the trespassory test applied in the majority's opinion reflects an irreducible constitutional minimum: When the Government physically invades personal property to gather information, a search occurs. The reaffirmation of that principle suffices to decide this case.

Nonetheless, as JUSTICE ALITO notes, physical intrusion is now unnecessary to many forms of surveillance. *Post,* at 9–12. With increasing regularity, the Government will be capable of duplicating the monitoring undertaken in this case by enlisting factory- or owner-installed vehicle tracking devices or GPS-enabled smart phones. See *United States* v. *Pineda-Moreno*, 617 F. 3d 1120, 1125 (CA9 2010) (Kozinski, C. J., dissenting from denial of rehearing en banc). In cases of electronic or other novel modes of surveillance that do not depend upon a physical invasion on property, the majority opinion's trespassory test may provide little guidance. But "[s]ituations involving merely the transmission of electronic signals without trespass would *remain* subject to *Katz* analysis." *Ante,* at 11. As JUSTICE ALITO incisively observes, the same technological advances that have made possible nontrespassory surveillance techniques will also affect the *Katz* test by shaping the evolution of societal privacy expectations. *Post,* at 10–11. Under that rubric, I agree with JUSTICE ALITO that, at the very least, "longer term GPS monitoring in investigations of most offenses impinges on expectations of privacy." *Post,* at 13.

In cases involving even short-term monitoring, some unique attributes of GPS surveillance relevant to the *Katz* analysis will require particular attention. GPS monitoring generates a precise, comprehensive record of a person's public movements that reflects a wealth of detail about her familial, political, professional, religious, and sexual associations. See, *e.g., People* v. *Weaver*, 12 N. Y. 3d 433, 441–442, 909 N. E. 2d 1195, 1199 (2009) ("Disclosed in [GPS] data . . . will be trips the indisputably private nature of which takes little imagination to conjure: trips to the psychiatrist, the plastic surgeon, the abortion clinic, the AIDS treatment center, the strip club, the criminal defense attorney, the by-the-hour motel, the union meeting, the mosque, synagogue or church, the gay bar and on and on"). The Government can store such records and efficiently mine them for information years into the future. *Pineda-Moreno*, 617 F. 3d, at 1124 (opinion of Kozinski, C. J.). And because GPS monitoring is cheap in comparison to conventional surveillance techniques and, by design, proceeds surreptitiously, it evades the ordinary checks that constrain abusive law enforcement practices:"limited police resources and community hostility." *Illinois* v. *Lidster*, 540 U. S. 419, 426 (2004).

Awareness that the Government may be watching chills associational and expressive freedoms. And the Government's unrestrained power to assemble data that reveal private aspects of identity is susceptible to abuse. The net result is that GPS monitoring—by making available at a relatively low cost such a substantial quantum of intimate information about any person whom the Government, in its unfettered discretion, chooses to track—may "alter the relationship between citizen and government in a way that is inimical to democratic society." *United States* v. *Cuevas-Perez*, 640 F. 3d 272, 285 (CA7 2011) (Flaum, J., concurring).

I would take these attributes of GPS monitoring into account when considering the existence of a reasonable societal expectation of privacy in the sum of one's public movements. I would ask whether people reasonably expect that their movements will be recorded and aggregated in a manner that enables the Government to ascertain, more or less at will, their political and religious beliefs, sexual habits, and so on. I do not regard as dispositive the fact that the Government might obtain the fruits of GPS monitoring through lawful conventional surveillance techniques. See *Kyllo*, 533 U. S., at 35, n. 2; *ante,* at 11 (leaving open the possibility that duplicating traditional surveillance "through electronic means, without an ac-companying trespass, is an unconstitutional invasion of privacy"). I would also consider the appropriateness of entrusting to the Executive, in the absence of any over-sight from a coordinate branch, a tool so amenable to misuse, especially in light of the Fourth Amendment's goal to curb arbitrary exercises of police power to and prevent "a too permeating police surveillance," *United States* v. *Di Re*, 332 U. S. 581, 595 (1948).*

More fundamentally, it may be necessary to reconsider the premise that an individual has no reasonable expectation of privacy in information voluntarily disclosed to third parties. *E.g., Smith*, 442 U. S., at 742; *United States* v. *Miller*, 425 U. S. 435, 443 (1976). This approach is ill suited to the digital age, in which people reveal a great deal of information about themselves to third parties in the course of carrying out mundane tasks. People disclose the phone numbers that they dial or text to their cellular providers; the URLs that they visit and the e-mail addresses with which they correspond to their Internet service providers; and the books, groceries, and medications they purchase to online retailers. Perhaps, as JUSTICE ALITO notes, some people may find the "tradeoff" of privacy for convenience "worthwhile," or come to accept this "diminution of privacy" as "inevitable," *post,* at 10, and perhaps not. I for one doubt that people would accept without complaint the warrantless disclosure to the Government of a list of every Web site they had visited in the last week, or month, or year. But whatever the societal expectations, they can attain constitutionally protected status only if our Fourth Amendment jurisprudence ceases to treat secrecy as a prerequisite for privacy. I would not assume that all information voluntarily disclosed to some member of the public for a limited purpose is, for that reason alone, disentitled to Fourth Amendment protection. See *Smith*, 442 U. S., at 749 (Marshall, J., dissenting) ("Privacy is not a discrete commodity, possessed absolutely or not at all. Those who disclose certain facts to a bank or phone company for a limited business purpose need not assume that this information will be released to other persons for other

* *United States* v. *Knotts*, 460 U. S. 276 (1983), does not foreclose the conclusion that GPS monitoring, in the absence of a physical intrusion, is a Fourth Amendment search. As the majority's opinion notes, *Knotts* reserved the question whether " 'different constitutional principles may be applicable' " to invasive law enforcement practices such as GPS tracking. See *ante,* at 8, n. 6 (quoting 460 U. S., at 284).

United States v. *Karo*, 468 U. S. 705 (1984), addressed the Fourth Amendment implications of the installation of a beeper in a container with the consent of the container's original owner, who was aware that the beeper would be used for surveillance purposes. *Id.,* at 707. Owners of GPS-equipped cars and smartphones do not contemplate that these devices will be used to enable covert surveillance of their movements. To the contrary, subscribers of one such service greeted a similar suggestion with anger. Quain, Changes to OnStar's Privacy Terms Rile Some Users, N. Y. Times (Sept. 22, 2011), online at http://wheels.blogs.nytimes.com/2011/09/22/changes-to-onstars-privacy-terms-rile-some-users (as visited Jan. 19, 2012, and available in Clerk of Court's case file). In addition, the bugged container in *Karo* lacked the close relationship with the target that a car shares with its owner. The bugged container in *Karo* was stationary for much of the Government's surveillance. See 468 U. S., at 708–710. A car's movements, by contrast, are its owner's movements.

purposes"); see also *Katz*, 389 U. S., at 351–352 ("[W]hat [a person] seeks to preserve as private, even in an area accessible to the public, may be constitutionally protected").

Resolution of these difficult questions in this case is unnecessary, however, because the Government's physical intrusion on Jones' Jeep supplies a narrower basis for decision. I therefore join the majority's opinion.

Alito, J., Concurring in Judgment

JUSTICE ALITO, with whom JUSTICE GINSBURG, JUSTICE BREYER, and JUSTICE KAGAN join, concurring in the judgment.

This case requires us to apply the Fourth Amendment's prohibition of unreasonable searches and seizures to a21st-century surveillance technique, the use of a Global Positioning System (GPS) device to monitor a vehicle's movements for an extended period of time. Ironically, the Court has chosen to decide this case based on 18th-century tort law. By attaching a small GPS device[9] to the under-side of the vehicle that respondent drove, the law enforcement officers in this case engaged in conduct that might have provided grounds in 1791 for a suit for trespass to chattels.[10] And for this reason, the Court concludes, the installation and use of the GPS device constituted a search. *Ante*, at 3–4.

This holding, in my judgment, is unwise. It strains the language of the Fourth Amendment; it has little if any support in current Fourth Amendment case law; and it is highly artificial.

I would analyze the question presented in this case by asking whether respondent's reasonable expectations of privacy were violated by the long-term monitoring of the movements of the vehicle he drove.

I

A

The Fourth Amendment prohibits "unreasonable searches and seizures," and the Court makes very little effort to explain how the attachment or use of the GPS device fits within these terms. The Court does not contend that there was a seizure. A seizure of property occurs when there is "some meaningful interference with an individual's possessory interests in that property," *United States* v. *Jacobsen,* 466 U. S. 109, 113 (1984), and here there was none.

Indeed, the success of the surveillance technique that the officers employed was dependent on the fact that the GPS did not interfere in any way with the operation of the vehicle, for if any such interference had been detected, the device might have been discovered.

The Court does claim that the installation and use of the GPS constituted a search, see *ante,* at 3–4, but this conclusion is dependent on the questionable proposition that these two procedures cannot be separated for purposes of Fourth Amendment analysis. If these two procedures are analyzed separately, it is not at all clear from the Court's opinion why either should be regarded as a search. It is clear that the attachment of the GPS device was not itself a search; if the device had not functioned or if the officers had not used it, no information would have been obtained. And the Court does not contend that the use of the device constituted a search either. On the contrary, the Court accepts the holding in *United States* v. *Knotts*, 460 U. S. 276 (1983), that the use of a surreptitiously planted electronic device to monitor a vehicle's movements on public roads did not amount to a search. See *ante*, at 7.

The Court argues—and I agree—that "we must 'assur[e]preservation of that degree of privacy against government that existed when the Fourth Amendment was adopted.' " *Ante*, at 5 (quoting *Kyllo* v. *United States*, 533 U. S. 27, 34 (2001)). But it is almost impossible to think of late- 18th-century situations that are analogous to what took place in this case. (Is it possible to imagine a case in which a constable secreted himself somewhere in a coach and remained there for a period of time in order to monitor the movements of the coach's owner?[11]) The Court's theory seems to be that the concept of a search, as originally understood, comprehended any technical trespass that led to the gathering of evidence, but we know that this is in-correct. At common law, any unauthorized intrusion on private property was actionable, see Prosser & Keeton 75,but a trespass on open fields, as opposed to the "curtilage" of a home, does not fall within the scope of the Fourth Amendment because private property outside the cartilage is not part of a "hous[e]" within the meaning of the Fourth Amendment. See *Oliver* v. *United States*, 466 U. S. 170 (1984); *Hester* v. *United States*, 265 U. S. 57 (1924).

B

The Court's reasoning in this case is very similar to that in the Court's early decisions involving wiretapping and electronic eavesdropping, namely, that a technical trespass followed by the gathering of evidence constitutes a search. In the early electronic surveillance cases, the Court concluded that a Fourth Amendment search occurred when private conversations were monitored as a result of an "unauthorized physical penetration into the premises occupied" by the defendant. *Silverman* v. *United States*, 365 U. S. 505, 509 (1961). In *Silverman*, police officers listened to conversations in an attached home by inserting a "spike mike" through the wall that this house shared with the vacant house next door. *Id.,* at 506. This procedure was held to be a search because the mike made contact with a heating duct on the other side of the wall and thus "usurp[ed] . . . an integral part of the premises." *Id.,* at 511.

By contrast, in cases in which there was no trespass, it was held that there was no search. Thus, in *Olmstead* v. *United States*, 277 U. S. 438 (1928), the Court found that the Fourth Amendment did not apply because "[t]he taps from house lines were made in the streets near the houses." *Id.*, at 457. Similarly, the Court concluded that no search occurred in *Goldman* v. *United States*, 316 U. S. 129, 135 (1942), where a "detectaphone" was placed on the outer wall of defendant's office for the purpose of overhearing conversations held within the room.

This trespass-based rule was repeatedly criticized. In *Olmstead*, Justice Brandeis wrote that it was "immaterial where the physical connection with the telephone wires was made." 277 U. S., at 479 (dissenting opinion). Al-though a private conversation transmitted by wire did not fall within the literal words of the Fourth Amendment, he argued, the Amendment should be understood as prohibiting "every unjustifiable intrusion by the government upon the privacy of the individual." *Id.,* at 478. See also, *e.g.*, *Silverman*, *supra*, at 513 (Douglas, J., concurring) ("The concept of 'an unauthorized physical penetration into the premises,' on which the present decision rests seems to me beside the point. Was not the wrong . . . done when the intimacies of the home were tapped, recorded, or revealed? The depth of the penetration of the electronic device—even the degree of its remoteness from the inside of the house—is not the measure of the injury"); *Goldman*, *supra*, at 139 (Murphy, J., dissenting) ("[T]he search of one's home or office no longer requires physical entry, for science has brought forth far more effective devices for the invasion of a person's privacy than the direct and obvious methods of oppression which were detested by our forebears and which inspired the Fourth Amendment").

Katz v. *United States*, 389 U. S. 347 (1967), finally did away with the old approach, holding that a trespass was not required for a Fourth Amendment violation. *Katz* involved the use of a listening device that was attached to the outside of a public telephone booth and that allowed police officers to eavesdrop on one end of the target's phone conversation. This procedure did not physically intrude on the area occupied by the target, but the *Katz* Court "repudiate[ed]" the old doctrine, *Rakas* v. *Illinois*, 439 U. S. 128, 143 (1978), and held that "[t]he fact that the electronic device employed . . . did not happen to penetrate the wall of the booth can have no constitutional significance," 389 U. S., at 353 ("[T]he reach of th[e] [Fourth] Amendment cannot turn upon the presence or absence of a physical intrusion into any given enclosure"); see *Rakas*, *supra*, at 143 (describing *Katz* as holding that the "capacity to claim the protection for the Fourth Amendment depends not upon a property right in the invaded place but upon whether the person who claims the protection of the Amendment has a legitimate expectation of privacy in the invaded place"); *Kyllo, supra,* at 32 ("We have since decoupled violation of a person's Fourth Amendment rights from trespassory violation of his property"). What mattered, the Court now held, was whether the conduct at issue "violated the privacy upon which [the defendant] justifiably relied while using the telephone booth." *Katz, supra*, at 353.

Under this approach, as the Court later put it when addressing the relevance of a technical trespass, "an actual trespass is neither necessary *nor sufficient* to establish a constitutional violation." *United States* v. *Karo,* 468 U. S. 705, 713 (1984) (emphasis added). *Ibid.* ("Com-par[ing] *Katz* v. *United States*, 389 U. S. 347 (1967) (no trespass, but Fourth Amendment violation), with *Oliver* v. *United States*, 466 U. S. 170 (1984) (trespass, but no Fourth Amendment violation)"). In *Oliver,* the Court wrote:

> "The existence of a property right is but one element in determining whether expectations of privacy are legitimate. 'The premise that property interests control the right of the Government to search and seize has been discredited.' *Katz*, 389 U. S., at 353, (quoting *Warden* v. *Hayden*, 387 U. S. 294, 304 (1967); some internal quotation marks omitted)." 466 U. S., at 183.

II

The majority suggests that two post-*Katz* decisions— *Soldal* v. *Cook County*, 506 U. S. 56 (1992), and *Alderman* v. *United States*, 394 U. S. 165 (1969)—show that a technical trespass is sufficient to establish the existence of a search, but they provide little support.

In *Soldal*, the Court held that towing away a trailer home without the owner's consent constituted a seizure even if this did not invade the occupants' personal privacy. But in the present case, the Court does not find that there was a seizure, and it is clear that none occurred.

In *Alderman,* the Court held that the Fourth Amendment rights of homeowners were implicated by the use of a surreptitiously planted listening device to monitor third-party conversations that occurred within their home. See 394 U. S., at 176–180. *Alderman* is best understood to mean that the homeowners had a legitimate expectation of privacy in all conversations that took place under their roof. See *Rakas*, 439 U. S., at 144, n. 12 (citing *Alderman* for the proposition that "the Court has not altogether abandoned use of property concepts in determining the presence or absence of the privacy interests protected by that Amendment"); 439 U. S., at 153 (Powell, J., concurring) (citing *Alderman* for the proposition that "property rights reflect society's explicit recognition of a person's authority to act as he wishes in certain areas, and there-fore should be considered in determining whether an individual's expectations of privacy are reasonable); *Karo*, *supra*, at 732 (Stevens, J., concurring in part and dissenting in part) (citing *Alderman* in support of the proposition that "a homeowner has a reasonable expectation of privacy in the contents of his home, including items owned by others").

In sum, the majority is hard pressed to find support in post-*Katz* cases for its trespass-based theory.

III

Disharmony with a substantial body of existing case law is only one of the problems with the Court's approach in this case.

I will briefly note four others. First, the Court's reasoning largely disregards what is really important (the *use* of a GPS for the purpose of long-term tracking) and instead attaches great significance to something that most would view as relatively minor (attaching to the bottom of a car a small, light object that does not interfere in any way with the car's operation). Attaching such an object is generally regarded as so trivial that it does not provide a basis for recovery under modern tort law. See Prosser & Keeton §14, at 87 (harmless or trivial contact with personal property not actionable); D. Dobbs, Law of Torts 124 (2000)(same). But under the Court's reasoning, this conduct may violate the Fourth Amendment. By contrast, if long-term monitoring can be accomplished without committing a technical trespass—suppose, for example, that the Federal Government required or persuaded auto manufacturers to include a GPS tracking device in every car—the Court's theory would provide no protection.

Second, the Court's approach leads to incongruous results. If the police attach a GPS device to a car and use the device to follow the car for even a brief time, under the Court's theory, the Fourth Amendment applies. But if the police follow the same car for a much longer period using unmarked cars and aerial assistance, this tracking is not subject to any Fourth Amendment constraints.

In the present case, the Fourth Amendment applies, the Court concludes, because the officers installed the GPS device after respondent's wife, to whom the car was registered, turned it over to respondent for his exclusive use. See *ante*, at 8. But if the GPS had been attached prior to that time, the Court's theory would lead to a different result. The Court proceeds on the assumption that respondent "had at least the property rights of a bailee," *ante*, at 3, n. 2, but a bailee may sue for a trespass to chattel only if the injury occurs during the term of the bailment. See 8A Am. Jur. 2d, Bailment §166, pp. 685– 686 (2009). So if the GPS device had been installed before respondent's wife gave him the keys, respondent would have no claim for trespass—and, presumably, no Fourth Amendment claim either.

Third, under the Court's theory, the coverage of the Fourth Amendment may vary from State to State. If the events at issue here had occurred in a community property State[12] or a State that has adopted the Uniform Marital Property Act,[13] respondent would likely be an owner of the vehicle, and it would not matter whether the GPS was installed before or after his wife turned over the keys. In non-community-property States, on the other hand, the registration of the vehicle in the name of respondent's wife would generally be regarded as presumptive evidence that she was the sole owner. See 60 C. J. S., Motor Vehicles §231, pp. 398–399 (2002); 8 Am. Jur. 2d, Automobiles §1208, pp. 859–860 (2007).

Fourth, the Court's reliance on the law of trespass will present particularly vexing problems in cases involving surveillance that is carried out by making electronic, as opposed to physical, contact with the item to be tracked. For example, suppose that the officers in the present case had followed respondent by surreptitiously activating a stolen vehicle detection system that came with the car when it was purchased. Would the sending of a radio signal to activate this system constitute a trespass to chattels? Trespass to chattels has traditionally required a physical touching of the property. See Restatement (Second) of Torts §217 and Comment *e* (1963 and 1964); Dobbs, *supra*, at

123. In recent years, courts have wrestled with the application of this old tort in cases involving unwanted electronic contact with computer systems, and some have held that even the transmission of electrons that occurs when a communication is sent from one computer to another is enough. See, *e.g., CompuServe, Inc.* v. *Cyber Promotions, Inc.* 962 F. Supp. 1015, 1021 (SD Ohio 1997); *Thrifty-Tel, Inc.* v. *Bezenek*, 46 Cal. App. 4th 1559, 1566, n. 6 (1996). But may such decisions be followed in applying the Court's trespass theory? Assuming that what matters under the Court's theory is the law of trespass as it existed at the time of the adoption of the Fourth Amendment, do these recent decisions represent a change in the law or simply the application of the old tort to new situations?

IV

A

The *Katz* expectation-of-privacy test avoids the problems and complications noted above, but it is not without its own difficulties. It involves a degree of circularity, see *Kyllo*, 533 U. S., at 34, and judges are apt to confuse their own expectations of privacy with those of the hypothetical reasonable person to which the *Katz* test looks. See *Minnesota* v. *Carter*, 525 U. S. 83, 97 (1998) (SCALIA, J., concurring). In addition, the *Katz* test rests on the assumption that this hypothetical reasonable person has a well-developed and stable set of privacy expectations. But technology can change those expectations. Dramatic technological change may lead to periods in which popular expectations are in flux and may ultimately produce significant changes in popular attitudes. New technology may provide increased convenience or security at the expense of privacy, and many people may find the tradeoff worthwhile. And even if the public does not welcome the diminution of privacy that new technology entails, they may eventually reconcile themselves to this development as inevitable.[14]

On the other hand, concern about new intrusions on privacy may spur the enactment of legislation to protect against these intrusions. This is what ultimately happened with respect to wiretapping. After *Katz*, Congress did not leave it to the courts to develop a body of Fourth Amendment case law governing that complex subject. Instead, Congress promptly enacted a comprehensive statute, see 18 U. S. C. §§2510–2522 (2006 ed. and Supp. IV), and since that time, the regulation of wiretapping has been governed primarily by statute and not by case law.[15] In an ironic sense, although *Katz* overruled *Olmstead*, Chief Justice Taft's suggestion in the latter case that the regulation of wiretapping was a matter better left for Congress, see 277 U. S., at 465–466, has been borne out.

B

Recent years have seen the emergence of many new devices that permit the monitoring of a person's movements. In some locales, closed-circuit television video monitoring is becoming ubiquitous. On toll roads, automatic toll collection systems create a precise record of the movements of motorists who choose to make use of that convenience. Many motorists purchase cars that are equipped with devices that permit a central station to ascertain the car's location at any time so that roadside assistance may be provided if needed and the car may be found if it is stolen.

Perhaps most significant, cell phones and other wireless devices now permit wireless carriers to track and record the location of users—and as of June 2011, it has been reported, there were more than 322 million wireless devices in use in the United States.[16] For older phones, the accuracy of the location information depends on the density of the tower network, but new "smart phones," which are equipped with a GPS device, permit more precise tracking. For example, when a user activates the GPS on such a phone, a provider is able to monitor the phone's location and speed of movement and can then report back real-time traffic conditions after combining ("crowdsourcing") the speed of all such phones on any particular road.[17] Similarly, phone-location-tracking services are offered as "social" tools, allowing consumers to find (or to avoid)others who enroll in these services. The availability and use of these and other new devices will continue to shape the average person's expectations about the privacy of his or her daily movements.

V

In the pre-computer age, the greatest protections of privacy were neither constitutional nor statutory, but practical. Traditional surveillance for any extended period of time was difficult and costly and therefore rarely undertaken. The surveillance at issue in this case—constant monitoring of the location of a vehicle for four weeks—would have required a large team of agents, multiple vehicles, and perhaps aerial assistance.[18] Only an investigation of unusual importance could have justified such an expenditure of law enforcement resources. Devices like the one used in the present case, however, make long-term monitoring relatively easy and cheap. In circumstances involving dramatic technological change, the best solution to privacy concerns may be legislative. See, *e.g.*, Kerr, 102 Mich. L. Rev., at 805–806. A legislative body is well situ-ated to gauge changing public attitudes, to draw detailed lines, and to balance privacy and public safety in a comprehensive way.

To date, however, Congress and most States have not enacted statutes regulating the use of GPS tracking tech-nology for law enforcement purposes. The best that we can do in this case is to apply existing Fourth Amendment doctrine and to ask whether the use of GPS tracking in aparticular case involved a degree of intrusion that a rea-sonable person would not have anticipated.

Under this approach, relatively short-term monitoring of a person's movements on public streets accords with expectations of privacy that our society has recognized as reasonable. See *Knotts,* 460 U. S., at 281–282. But the use of longer term GPS monitoring in investigations of most offenses impinges on expectations of privacy. For such offenses, society's expectation has been that law enforcement agents and others would not—and indeed, in the main, simply could not—secretly monitor and catalogue every single movement of an individual's car for a very long period. In this case, for four weeks, law enforcement agents tracked every movement that respondent made in the vehicle he was driving. We need not identify with precision the point at which the tracking of this vehicle became a search, for the line was surely crossed before the 4-week mark. Other cases may present more difficult questions. But where uncertainty exists with respect to whether a certain period of GPS surveil lance is long enough to constitute a Fourth Amendment search, the police may always seek a warrant.[19] We also need not consider whether prolonged GPS monitoring in the context of investigations involving extraordinary offenses would similarly intrude on a constitutionally protected sphere of privacy. In such cases, long-term tracking might have been mounted using previously available techniques.

For these reasons, I conclude that the lengthy monitoring that occurred in this case constituted a search under the Fourth Amendment. I therefore agree with the majority that the decision of the Court of Appeals must be affirmed.

End Notes

[1] In this litigation, the Government has conceded noncompliance with the warrant and has argued only that a warrant was not required. *United States* v. *Maynard*, 615 F. 3d 544, 566, n. (CADC 2010).

[2] As we have noted, the Jeep was registered to Jones's wife. The Government acknowledged, however, that Jones was "the exclusive driver." *Id.*, at 555, n. (internal quotation marks omitted). If Jones was not the owner he had at least the property rights of a bailee. The Court of Appeals concluded that the vehicle's registration did not affect his ability to make a Fourth Amendment objection, *ibid.*, and the Government has not challenged that determination here. We therefore do not consider the Fourth Amendment significance of Jones's status.

[3] JUSTICE ALITO'S concurrence (hereinafter concurrence) doubts the wisdom of our approach because "it is almost impossible to think of late-18th-century situations that are analogous to what took place in this case." *Post*, at 3 (opinion concurring in judgment). But in fact it posits a situation that is not far afield—a constable's concealing himself in the target's coach in order to track its movements. *Ibid.* There is no doubt that the information gained by that trespassory activity would be the product of an unlawful search—whether that information consisted of the conversations occurring in the coach, or of the destinations to which the coach traveled.

In any case, it is quite irrelevant whether there was an 18th-centuryanalog. Whatever new methods of investigation may be devised, our task, *at a minimum*, is to decide whether the action in question would have constituted a "search" within the original meaning of the Fourth Amendment. Where, as here, the Government obtains information by physically intruding on a constitutionally protected area, such a search has undoubtedly occurred.

[4] Thus, the concurrence's attempt to recast *Alderman* as meaning that individuals have a "legitimate expectation of privacy in all conversations that [take] place under their roof," *post*, at 6–7, is foreclosed by the Court's opinion. The Court took as a given that the homeowner's "conversational privacy" had not been violated.

[5] The concurrence notes that post-*Katz* we have explained that " 'an actual trespass is neither necessary *nor sufficient* to establish a constitutional violation.' " *Post*, at 6 (quoting *United States* v. *Karo*, 468 U. S. 705, 713 (1984)). That is undoubtedly true, and undoubtedly irrelevant. *Karo* was considering whether a seizure occurred, and as the concurrence explains, a seizure of property occurs, not when there is a trespass, but "when there is some meaningful interference with an individual's possessory interests in that property." *Post*, at 2 (internal quotation marks omitted). Likewise with a search. Trespass alone does not qualify, but there must be conjoined with that what was present here: an attempt to find something or to obtain information.

Related to this, and similarly irrelevant, is the concurrence's point that, if analyzed separately, neither the installation of the device nor its use would constitute a Fourth Amendment search. See *ibid.* Of course not. A trespass on "houses" or "effects," or a *Katz* invasion of privacy, is not alone a search unless it is done to obtain information; and the obtaining of information is not alone a search unless it is achieved by such a trespass or invasion of privacy.

[6] *Knotts* noted the "limited use which the government made of the signals from this particular beeper," 460 U. S., at 284; and reserved the question whether "different constitutional principles may be applicable" to "dragnet-type law enforcement practices" of the type that GPS tracking made possible here, *ibid.*

[7] The Government also points to *Cardwell* v. *Lewis*, 417 U. S. 583 (1974), in which the Court rejected the claim that the inspection of an impounded vehicle's tire tread and the collection of paint scrapings from its exterior violated the Fourth Amendment. Whether the plurality said so because no search occurred or because the search was reasonable is unclear.

Compare *id.*, at 591 (opinion of Blackmun, J.)("[W]e fail to comprehend what expectation of privacy was infringed"), with *id.*, at 592 ("Under circumstances such as these, where probable cause exists, a warrantless examination of the exterior of a car is not unreasonable . . .").

[8] Thus, our theory is *not* that the Fourth Amendment is concerned with "*any* technical trespass that led to the gathering of evidence." *Post*, at 3 (ALITO, J., concurring in judgment) (emphasis added). The Fourth Amendment protects against trespassory searches only with regard to those items ("persons, houses, papers, and effects") that it enumerates. The trespass that occurred in *Oliver* may properly be understood as a "search," but not one "in the constitutional sense." 466 U. S., at 170, 183.

[9] Although the record does not reveal the size or weight of the device used in this case, there is now a device in use that weighs two ounces and is the size of a credit card. Tr. of Oral Arg. 27.

[10] At common law, a suit for trespass to chattels could be maintained if there was a violation of "the dignitary interest in the inviolability of chattels," but today there must be "some actual damage to the chattel before the action can be maintained." W. Keeton, D. Dobbs, R. Keeton, & D. Owen, Prosser & Keeton on Law of Torts 87 (5th ed. 1984) (here-inafter Prosser & Keeton). Here, there was no actual damage to the vehicle to which the GPS device was attached.

[11] The Court suggests that something like this might have occurred in 1791, but this would have required either a gigantic coach, a very tiny constable, or both—not to mention a constable with incredible fortitude and patience.

[12] See, *e.g.*, Cal. Family Code Ann. §760 (West 2004).

[13] See Uniform Marital Property Act §4, 9A U. L. A. 116 (1998).

[14] See, *e.g.*, NPR, The End of Privacy http://www.npr.org/series/114250076/the-end-of-privacy (all Internet materials as visited Jan. 20, 2012, and available in Clerk of Court's case file); Time Magazine, Everything About You Is Being Tracked—Get Over It, Joel Stein, Mar.21, 2011, Vol. 177, No. 11.

[15] See Kerr, The Fourth Amendment and New Technologies: Constitutional Myths and the Case for Caution, 102 Mich. L. Rev. 801, 850–851(2004) (hereinafter Kerr).

[16] See CTIA Consumer Info, 50 Wireless Quick Facts, http://www.ctia.org/consumer_info/index.cfm/AID/10323.

[17] See, *e.g.*, The bright side of sitting in traffic: Crowdsourcing road congestion data, Google Blog, http://googleblog.blogspot.com/2009/08/bright-side-of-sitting-in-traffic.html.

[18] Even with a radio transmitter like those used in *United States* v. *Knotts*, 460 U. S. 276 (1983), or *United States* v. *Karo,* 468 U. S. 705 (1984), such long-term surveillance would have been exceptionally demanding. The beepers used in those cases merely "emit[ted] periodic signals that [could] be picked up by a radio receiver." *Knotts*, 460 U.S., at 277. The signal had a limited range and could be lost if the police did not stay close enough. Indeed, in *Knotts* itself, officers lost the signal from the beeper, and only "with the assistance of a monitoring device located in a helicopter [was] the approximate location of the signal . . . picked up again about one hour later." *Id.*, at 278.

[19] In this case, the agents obtained a warrant, but they did not comply with two of the warrant's restrictions: They did not install the GPS device within the 10-day period required by the terms of the warrant and by Fed. Rule Crim. Proc. 41(e)(2)(B)(i), and they did not install the GPS device within the District of Columbia, as required by the terms of the warrant and by 18 U. S. C. §3117(a) and Rule 41(b)(4). In the courts below the Government did not argue, and has not argued here, that the Fourth Amendment does not impose these precise restrictions and that the violation of these restrictions does not demand the suppression of evidence obtained using the tracking device. See, *e.g., United States* v. *Gerber*, 994 F. 2d 1556, 1559–1560 (CA11 1993); *United States* v. *Burke*, 517 F. 2d 377, 386–387 (CA2 1975). Because it was not raised, that question is not before us.

INDEX

D

E

M

N

O

P

Q

R

U

V

W